# The Bush Survival Bible

# The
# Bush
# Survival
# Bible

*250 Ways to Make It Through the Next Four Years*
*Without Misunderestimating the Dangers Ahead,*
*and Other Subliminable Strategeries*

## Gene Stone

VILLARD  NEW YORK

*The Bush Survival Bible* is a work of nonfiction. It is not, however, intended as a substitute for professional medical, financial, travel, or any other kind of advice from any other kind of professional. Furthermore, the sites to which readers are referred on the "Internets" are subject to change, and the author and publisher make no representation as to the accuracy or dependability of any site referred to in this book, or any information on any such site, or anything else, for that matter. Finally, the reader is reminded that while "Bushisms" are actual attempts at coherent speech by George W. Bush, the jokes are just actual attempts at jokes.

Published in the United States by Villard Books, an imprint of The Random House Publishing Group, a division of Random House, Inc., New York.

VILLARD and "V" CIRCLED Design are registered trademarks of Random House, Inc.

Library of Congress Cataloging-in-Publication Data is available.

ISBN 0-8129-7476-X

Printed in the United States of America

Villard Books website address: www.villard.com

987654321

First Edition

*This book is dedicated to everyone who voted
for John F. Kerry*

# CONTENTS

INTRODUCTION    xi

6 Tips to Maintain Your Sanity    3
*by Judith Orloff*

7 Points from the Left of Liberal    5
*by Robert Anbian*

9 Groups to Join    9

6 Ways to Get Involved in Local Politics    16
*by Gale A. Brewer*

5 Rising Stars to Watch    19

10 Progressive Movers, Shakers, and Writers    25

9 People Worse Than Bush
(in no particular order)    30

7 American Politicians More Frightening
Than Bush    36

9 New Drinks to Get You By    42

7 Tips for Women    43
*by Gail Evans*

**10 Retrofitted Movies for Republicans**   47

**10 Things Parents Can Say to Their Children**   48
*by James Howe*

**10 Ways to Make Money**   50
*by Russell Pearlman*

**6 Republican Reality TV Shows to Keep You Busy**   56

**8 Topics to Inspire Writers**   58
*by Tracy Kidder*

**7 Media Habits of Highly Effective People
Who Aren't Republican**   62
*by Kurt Andersen*

**6 Reasons to Love Global Warming**   65

**1 Internet Rule to Remember**   66
*by Tim Sanders*

**11 Books That Will Make You Feel Better,
Wiser, or More Wistful**   68

**6 Pieces of Music to Transport You
to Another World**   72

**7 Anti-Bush Movies**   74

**8 Games to Play with Bush's Body**   78

**7 Countries to Move to**   82

**8 Excuses for Being Late to Work**   88

**13 Ways to Pass as a Republican**   89

**5 Great Golf Courses**   92
*by John Paul Newport*

13 Steps to Protect Your Body  96
*by Mark Liponis*

4 Treatments to Make Your Body Feel Better  100

5 Lovable Dog Breeds to Adopt  103
*by the Winnipeg Humane Society*

2 Mental Health Strategies  107

6 Reflections on Depression  109
*by Andrew Solomon*

5 Excellent Antidepressants  111

7 Modern Virtues to Live By  114
*by Anita L. Allen*

1 Way to Tell If Bush Is Lying  116

9 Prayers to Get You Through the Night  118
*by Timothy Dobbins*

# INTRODUCTION

We are worried about you. Yes, you—you with the ashen face, pale lips, and expression of dazed horror.

The election is over, and you have just been presented with one of the more severe diagnoses of your lifetime: Bush won. You must suffer through four more years.

Now what? Despair? Despondency? Grief?

In truth, if you are to adjust to your fate, there are four stages you will need to pass through.

The first stage is denial: "It didn't really happen. It couldn't have. Kerry won. If I close my eyes hard and open them again, I'll wake up. This is a bad dream."

No, it's reality. Get used to it. You have to live in the real world, because if you don't, things will stop making sense and only get worse.

For example, denial may lead you to forget the facts of your past and replace them with a fantasy, like the one in which you're a military hero instead of a draft dodger. Or even worse, you may become delusional about your finances, spending wildly beyond your means and racking up so much debt that there's no hope of ever repaying it.

The second stage is anger—irrational, self-righteous fury. You'll have to fight to restrain it. Unchecked, it may lead you to trash people's constitutional rights or become paranoid enough to attack them in order to preempt future harm. You might even go as far as destroying the very place you live, through a deranged effort to control it.

Even worse, you may declare war on a country that just happens to bother you.

The third stage is a kind of bland stupidity. Here you lose control of even the most basic intellectual faculties. The first sign is that you stop reading books and newspapers. In fact, the only way you'll seek any outside information is secondhand, through friends who are afraid of you.

Soon, you'll lose the ability to pronounce multi-syllabic words—or even construct basic sentences. At its worst, during this phase you'll even lose bodily functions, like the ability to swallow pretzels without gagging.

The final, and thus most important, stage is coping and recovery. That's what this book is about.

This is no time for denial, anger, or stupidity. Other people have perfected those traits, and you won't be able to compete. Instead, this is the moment to grasp reality, get past rage, smarten up, and choose a course of action.

Many choices are provided here: You can escape to another country or get a new hobby. You can campaign for Bush's replacement or run for office yourself. You can listen to music, watch movies, or read a book. You can take a pill, take a voyage, or take time off. You can eat, drink, or store your blood in a hospital. You can hypnotize yourself into believing that someone else is president, or you can Google authority.

Whatever you choose, remember that you're not alone. Nearly every thinking person in this country is now suffering from a form of postelection stress disorder.

That's why this book can help. Read it thoroughly. Take some action. Create a community of like-minded citizens. But you must do something for your soul, for your country, and for the soul of your country.

Gene Stone and the *Bush Survival Bible* Team:
        Carl Pritzkat
        Tony Travostino
        Christopher Barillas
        Sarah Albert
        Miranda Spencer

November 2004

# The Bush Survival Bible

# 6 Tips to Maintain Your Sanity

*Judith Orloff*

*Judith Orloff, M.D., the author of* Positive Energy: 10 Extraordinary Prescriptions for Transforming Fatigue, Stress, and Fear into Vibrance, Strength, & Love *(Harmony Books, 2004), is an assistant clinical professor of psychiatry at UCLA. Visit her website at www.judithorloff.com.*

Before you do anything else, make sure you stay sane. Sanity is more important than ever, so follow these tips.

1. Don't let yourself be overcome with fear. Bush won because he played the fear card—he ran on fear; he rules on fear. But fear creates negative energy—in you and in others around you. Don't feed into this outright manipulation of your emotions. Just say no to fear. Instead, feel joy, or hope, or love. Don't let them make you feel afraid.

2. Guard against energy vampires. These are people who suck your energy dry. Instead of talking to people

who are stuck on the negatives surrounding the election, surround yourself with positive people who can talk about how to create change.

3. Counter the stress. Try a three-minute break. Take a breath, close your eyes, inhale, exhale, and if negative thoughts occur, focus on the breath and visualize something very positive, such as a free world, or peace, or a good president.

4. Avoid techno-despair. Don't be overwhelmed by information overload. Take some breaks from CNN and online news now and then. You're not a news anchor. You don't need to know what's going on every minute.

5. Stay in the now. Instead of catastrophizing about the future, focus on the here and now. Be kind to yourself. Take a moment off. Look around at the sky, the birds, and the sunlight. Think about something other than the presidency.

6. Always be of anonymous service. Keep giving. Spread the energy around. Leave small amounts of money in public places. Create happy surprises for others. Don't just wait for the big opportunities, or you may never do anything at all.

# 7 Points from the Left of Liberal

*Robert Anbian*

*Poet and journalist Robert Anbian is the founder of ProtestWorks.com, a propaganda enterprise spreading peace and justice messages while donating profits to activists. He has published four poetry collections, most recently* WE Parts 1 & 2 *(Night Horn Books, 1999) and* Blame the Powerful *(War&Peace Press, 2004). He lives in San Francisco with his wife, Nona Bailey.*

1. Be politically nonsectarian. Embrace the broadest possible front of all sane and fair-minded people in resistance to the rising tide of war, terror, and oppression. We have to reject the right-wing nuts once and for all. There are many sane and fair-minded conservatives, middle-of-the-roaders, and usually-don't-give-a-damners who will join this effort.

2. Don't despair. Don't give up. Don't get disgusted with politics. Politics is how a society makes up its mind. There's no reason the process should be any more neat, calm, or noble than your own mind's processes.

So stop whining, hitch up your pants, and get on with it.

3. Resist and oppose. Get active. You are not required to be a saint, an ideologue, a purist, or a full-time activist to make a difference. You need to do whatever is in your power that is realistic and sustainable and has a chance of having practical effect. You'll feel a lot better for doing it.

4. Forget being apologetic for preaching to the choir. It's called energizing the base, and it's just as important for progressives as for right-wing nuts.

5. Get involved before and beyond elections. Bush the Junior's reelection is proof ours is a managed democracy at best. By the time elections roll around, the fix is more or less in. Pay special attention to senators and congresspeople who are voting year-round. Write yours at least twice a year, especially when major issues are at stake. Attend at least one hometown appearance by your senator or representative; ask him or her a question; hand him or her one of your letters. If you visit Washington, make an appointment, even if only to speak to an aide. Form letters, circular e-mails, and the like have some effect, but the personal touch counts. If your senator and representative are good folk, don't go to sleep on supporting them. Look for a contested congressional district or a Senate seat in your region that might swing progressive and give whatever money, time, or other support you can.

6. Don't cooperate with unwarranted, intrusive, and intimidating police action. You don't have to answer anyone's questions or show them anything, and if you are being held or compelled in any way, remember that you have the right to a lawyer.

At a party a man came up to Texas governor George W. Bush and said, "Have you heard the latest George W. Bush joke?"

Governor Bush said, "I'm George W Bush."

The man said, "Oh, I'll tell it slowly."

**BUSHISM:**
**"Families is where our nation finds hope, where wings take dream."**

—LaCrosse, Wisconsin, October 18, 2000

7. Don't lose your joy. Here, now, in the life we live, are all the rejuvenating experiences that give us hope: love, sensual pleasure, the snap of understanding, the magic of imagination, collective struggle. In joy are the reasons and means to reject fear, hate, poverty, and the terrors of war. No shit.

# 9 Groups to Join

As they say, now is the time for all good men to come to the aid of the party. And all good women, too.

1. MoveOn (www.moveon.org)

   *Mission:* Bring ordinary people back into politics; be a catalyst for a new kind of grassroots involvement, supporting busy but concerned citizens in finding their political voice.

   Founded in 1998 by two Silicon Valley entrepreneurs (part of the team that created the *Flying Toasters* screen saver) to protest Bill Clinton's impeachment, MoveOn ballooned in popularity in the lead-up to the Iraq war and was largely responsible for the turnout to the antiwar protests in 2003. It now boasts more than two million members and spends tens of millions of dollars on its issues and candidates—making it the ten-thousand-pound gorilla in left-wing politics and a favorite target of the right. MoveOn has pioneered innovative ways of involving masses of people in the political process, including online phone banks, ad idea contests, and instant ad development.

2. America Coming Together
   (ACT, www.actforvictory.org)

   *Mission:* Energize the electorate to achieve crucial changes—the mobilization of millions of people to register and vote, the defeat of George W. Bush and his Republican allies, and the election of progressives in important state, local, and federal contests.

   ACT was founded in the lead-up to the 2004 presidential election with the goal of becoming the largest and most sophisticated voter mobilization project in American history. Its founders, veterans of such groups as Emily's List, Sierra Club, the AFL-CIO, and the Democratic National Committee, built the organization to facilitate alliances with existing organizations on the left. The nucleus of ACT is America Votes, a coalition of more than thirty national get-out-the-vote organizations focused on progressive issues like the environment, civil and human rights, women's rights, reproductive choice, education, and labor. The organization offers a wide variety of ways to become engaged both online and in local areas.

3. Democracy for America
   (DFA, www.democracyforamerica.com)

   *Mission:* Support fiscally responsible, socially progressive candidates at all levels of government, from the school board to the presidency.

   Democracy for America took the infrastructure and initials of Howard Dean's revolutionary presidential campaign, Dean for America, and shifted it into an ongoing movement, with Dean still in the lead. Hoping to keep the interest of the young and disinterested voters that responded so well to the Dean candidacy, DFA is big on adopting local candidates and using the tools the original DFA so effectively created: blogging, meet-ups, and house parties.

4. People For the American Way (www.pfaw.org)

*Mission:* Meet the challenges of discord and fragmentation with an affirmation of "the American Way"—pluralism; individuality; freedom of thought, expression, and religion; a sense of community; and tolerance and compassion for others.

People For the American Way was founded in 1981 by Norman Lear, Barbara Jordan, Father Theodore Hesburgh, and Andrew Heiskell as a response to the rise of the religious right. Since then it has been one of the most consistent and steadfast forces opposing the right wing. And in a twenty-three-year period that included both Bush administrations and eight years of Ronald Reagan, that's saying a lot. In the 1980s it was revolutionary in its use of TV ads to shape public opinion on social issues, and it was instrumental in blocking the appointment of Robert Bork to the Supreme Court. In the 1990s it was a major force countering the Christian Coalition and the Clinton impeachment, and since 2000 it has fought the Bush agenda every step of the way. While less in-your-face than its younger cousin MoveOn, it is much broader in its scope and offers many effective ways to participate, especially through letter writing.

5. Wellstone Action! (www.wellstone.org)

*Mission:* Continue Paul and Sheila Wellstone's fight for economic justice and progressive social change.

Wellstone Action! was founded in 2002 after

Minnesota senator Paul Wellstone and his wife, Sheila, were killed in a plane crash just two weeks before the election in which he was running for a third term as the Democratic senator from Minnesota. Wellstone's children founded the organization to carry on his populist approach to progressive politics. The organization offers a wide range of tools for getting active, whether volunteering for local campaigns, grassroots organizing, and networking around progressive issues or participating in training sessions for grassroots organizing.

6. Sierra Club (www.sierraclub.org)

*Mission:* Explore, enjoy, and protect the wild places of the Earth. Practice and promote the responsible use of the Earth's ecosystems and resources. Educate and enlist humanity to protect and restore the quality of the natural and human environment.

Over one hundred years old, with more than seven hundred thousand members, the Sierra Club has helped establish Yosemite National Park and Yellowstone National Park, and it helped pass the Alaska National Interest Lands Conservation Act designating more than one hundred million acres of parks, wildlife refuges, and wilderness areas. As its website reveals, the organization is well equipped to engage all of its members in activism on a wide range of environmental issues. And when the e-mailing, letter writing and phone lobbying get tiresome, there is always the environment itself—the club offers many enjoyable ways to appreciate it.

7. League of Women Voters (www.lwv.org)

*Mission:* Encourage the informed and active participation of citizens in government, work to increase understanding of major public policy issues, and influence public policy through education and advocacy.

Founded six months before women had the right to vote (in 1920), the league has remained nonpartisan and committed to concepts like diversity and participation—principles that have left the organization out of favor with the Bush administration. The league has one of the most developed networks of local and statewide leagues, offering incredible opportunities for real, in-the-flesh involvement. They also employ the standard virtual tools, such as e-mail lists and letter writing.

8. Progressive Majority (www.progressivemajority.org)

*Mission:* Elect progressive champions who will help change the direction of this country by building a nationwide member network that provides much-needed early support to progressive candidates.

Progressive Majority, a subgroup of the Democratic Party, is a group of more than thirty progressive Democrats in Congress hoping to generate funds for progressive candidates. Although their website has some of the usual trappings of activist sites, such as e-mail newsletters and letter-writing campaigns, the main focus is to raise money for progressive candidates.

9. New Democrat Network (NDN, www.newdem.org)

*Mission:* Modernize progressive politics, build a new and durable Democratic majority, and advocate for an agenda that will create a better future for our children.

Closely aligned with the Democratic Party, New Democrat Network was founded in 1996 as part of the new wave of institutions trying to build an infra-

George W. Bush, running as the pro-education candidate, made many campaign stops at grade schools where he posed for pictures while reading to kids or chatting with them in class. At one photo-op stop, a teacher was giving a lesson on the circulation of the blood.

Dubya chimed in, possibly trying to make the teacher's lesson clearer. He said, "Now, children, if I stood on my head the blood, as you know, would run into it, and I would turn red in the face."

"Yes, sir," one of the girls said.

"Then why is it that while I am standing upright the blood doesn't run into my feet?"

A small voice piped up from the back of the room shouted, "'Cause your feet aren't empty."

**BUSHISM:**
"Listen, Al Gore is a very tough opponent. He is the incumbent. He represents the incumbency. And a challenger is somebody who generally comes from the pack and wins, if you're going to win. And that's where I'm coming from."

—Detroit, September 7, 2000

structure for legitimizing progressive politics—in the same way organizations like the Heritage Foundation and the American Enterprise Institute have done for conservatism. The group reaches out to disenfranchised voters in concerted campaigns like its Hispanic Project. It places ads to influence public opinion and it endorses candidates, providing them money and support. Additionally, it operates its own progressive think tank.

# 6 Ways to Get Involved in Local Politics

*Gale A. Brewer*

*Gale A. Brewer represents the Upper West Side and Clinton neighborhoods in the New York City Council, where she chairs the Committee on Technology in Government. She has received numerous awards from more than two dozen neighborhood and nonprofit boards and has taught urban policy at Barnard, Baruch, Brooklyn, Hunter, and Queens colleges.*

Local politics becomes even more important when the national election takes a bad turn. When your president doesn't seem to care about your issues and federal aid begins to dry up, you need local officials who will pick up the slack. Just today, for instance, our council met to discuss transportation; the federal government hasn't been responsive to our needs so we're going to have to find funding from state and local sources. These sources have never been more important. So find a way to get involved in your local political arena.

1. Campaign. Find someone you like, and do some campaign work. It's best to choose a political figure whose election results are in doubt rather than someone who's going to breeze to a victory. As much as you might like your city council member, someone else might need your help more.

   While campaigning, you'll learn about the political clubs, press conferences, celebrity endorsements, labor unions, and more. You'll develop an address book of people and contacts, which means that the next time you're working for a candidate or an issue, or running your own campaign, you'll have a superb list of names you can call on.

2. Become an expert in a specific area. For example, there's an organization in New York called the Straphangers Campaign that has become the authority on mass transit. Their surveys and research are taken seriously by everyone, and they have a powerful effect on policy. Find something you care about and become the local authority.

3. Run for a place in your local civic group or community board. These little city halls, supported by minimal staff, are where citizens in the neighborhood learn about and legislate issues such as zoning, affordable housing, and the size of buildings. They can be a stepping-stone to future political positions, but they can also be rewarding in themselves.

4. Testify. When you feel strongly about an issue, go to your civic group, community board, or city council meeting and testify. Whether it's because you don't think there's enough handicapped parking, adequate after-school programs, or a stoplight on your street

corner, start your political career by speaking out at a forum where they want to hear from you, and where you could make a difference.

5. Intern. Seek out an official and volunteer to be part of the organization. Few local politicians have adequate staffs, and they may quickly be able to put you to work in interesting ways.

6. Write a position paper. All politicians need them, but local officials seldom have the staff to develop as much solid material as they'd like. You may be able to present the paper yourself at a press conference or with your chosen politician. A good position paper on how to get rid of graffiti or how to improve public transport, for example, will always be valuable and appreciated.

# 5 Rising Stars to Watch

Apart from the three Democrats credited with being early hopefuls in the 2008 presidential race, Senator Hillary Clinton, retired general Wesley Clark, and former vice presidential candidate John Edwards, many others are making names for themselves and doing good works in Democratic circles, getting the attention of national party power brokers. All have demonstrated the ability to cross political lines and expand the party's effectiveness and appeal.

1.  Representative Stephanie Herseth

    Representative Stephanie Herseth of South Dakota is a young Democrat who is generating a lot of excitement. In June 2004 she won a close House race to replace Representative Bill Janklow, a Republican who was convicted of manslaughter for a 2003 traffic accident.

    Now thirty-three, Herseth grew up on her family's farm and ranch near Houghton, in the northeast-

While visiting England, George Bush is invited to tea with the queen. He asks her what her leadership philosophy is. She says that it is to surround herself with intelligent people. He asks how she knows if they're intelligent.

"By asking them the right questions," says the queen. "Allow me to demonstrate."

She phones Tony Blair and says, "Mr. Prime Minister. Please answer this question: Your mother has a child, and your father has a child, and this child is not your brother or sister. Who is it?"

Tony Blair responds, "It's me, ma'am."

"Correct. Thank you and goodbye, sir," says the queen. She hangs up and says, "Did you get that, Mr. Bush?"

"Yes ma'am. Thanks a lot. I'll definitely be using that!"

Upon returning to Washington, he decides he'd better put the Senate majority leader to the test. He summons Trent Lott to the White House and says, "Senator Lott, I wonder if you can answer a question for me."

"Why, of course, sir. What's on your mind?"

"Uhh, your mother has a child, and your father has a child, and this child is not your brother or your sister. Who is it?"

Lott hems and haws and finally asks, "Can I think about it and get back to you?"

Bush agrees, and Lott leaves. He immediately calls a meeting of other senior Republican senators, and they puzzle over the question for several hours, but nobody can come up with an answer. Finally, in desperation, Lott calls Colin Powell at the State Department and explains his problem.

"Now lookee here, son, your mother has a child, and your father has a child, and this child is not your brother or your sister. Who is it?"

Powell answers immediately, "It's me, of course."

Much relieved, Lott rushes back to the White House and exclaims, "I know the answer, sir! I know who it is! It's Colin Powell!"

And Bush replies in disgust, "Wrong, you dumb shit, it's Tony Blair!"

**BUSHISM:**
"Our priorities is our faith."

—Greensboro, North Carolina, October 10, 2000

ern part of the state, and attended Georgetown University in Washington, D.C., where she graduated summa cum laude and Phi Beta Kappa with a B.A. in government. Herseth received her law degree from the Georgetown University Law Center, was a senior editor of the law review, and served on the faculty in 1997.

Herseth comes from a long line of South Dakota politicians. Her grandfather Ralph Herseth was governor from 1959 to 1961, and her grandmother Lorna served as South Dakota's secretary of state. Her father, Lars, was a twenty-year veteran of the state legislature who unsuccessfully ran for governor in 1986.

2. Representative Tim Ryan

On January 7, 2003, Representative Tim Ryan was sworn in as the youngest Democratic member of the 108th Congress. The first freshman representative in his congressional class to speak on the House floor, Congressman Ryan has quickly proven himself to be a strong and inspirational leader in the House of Representatives.

An October 2004 speech spoke directly to young people's fears about a postelection draft. The Ohio Democrat said it was little wonder that Americans viewed with skepticism assurances from the Bush administration that no draft was forthcoming. Such assurances, he said, "came from the people who told us Saddam Hussein had something to do with 9/11; the same people who told us Saddam Hussein had weapons of mass destruction; the same people who told us we were going to be able to use the oil for reconstruction money; the same people who told us that we'd be greeted as liberators, not occupiers; the same president that told us the Taliban is gone; the same president that told us that Poland is our ally, two days before they pull out; same president that tells us Iraq is going just great; same president that tells us the economy is going just great; same people that told us the tax cut was gonna create millions of jobs; same people that told us that the Medicare program only cost 400 billion dollars, when it really cost 540 billion dollars—so please forgive us for not believing what you're saying! Please forgive the students of this country for not believing what you're saying!"

3. Senator Barack Obama

Barack Obama, whose father was from Kenya and his mother from Kansas, was born and raised in Hawaii and until the start of the 2004 election season was a little-known Illinois state senator. Obama attended Harvard Law School, becoming the first African American president of the prestigious *Harvard Law Review*. Praised for his charisma, intellect, and devotion to progressive ideals, Obama graduated from Harvard and moved to Chicago, to work as a community organizer on the city's hardscrabble South Side. He practiced civil rights law before serving in the state senate. He also has taught at the University of Chicago Law School and wrote a memoir, *Dreams from My Father* (Three Rivers Press, 2004).

"I think that my first job is to represent all of the people of Illinois—black, white, Hispanic, Asian, rural, urban—and to make sure I understand the process and I'm delivering for them," Obama told CNN during his race for the U.S. Senate. "But I welcome the opportunity to serve, perhaps, as a role model for African American young people who aspire to public office, and I welcome the opportunity to help frame the debate in terms of how we move away from a racially polarized society toward one that is actually going to be good for all people."

A self-described "skinny guy from the South Side with a funny name," his electrifying keynote speech at the Democratic National Convention in 2004 immediately propelled him to the top ranks of the party, a new, powerful voice that spoke to the best and the brightest of the party's fundamental ideals. Having been elected to the U.S. Senate, Obama has a national platform to showcase his talents and hone new skills.

4. Elliot Spitzer

Since he took over as New York State's sixty-third attorney general on January 1, 1999, Spitzer has become one of the most dynamic attorneys general in the nation's history, having pushed initiatives to make New York a national leader in investor protection, environmental stewardship, labor rights, personal privacy, public safety, and criminal law enforcement.

Spitzer's investigations of conflicts of interest on Wall Street have been the catalyst for dramatic reform in the nation's financial services industry, and he shows no sign of slowing down.

Spitzer spearheaded efforts to bring lawsuits against midwestern and mid-Atlantic power plants responsible for acid rain and smog in the Northeast. His prosecution of white-collar corruption and crime in the financial services and insurance sectors has resulted in broad-reaching reforms and some of the nation's largest fraud recoveries. Through this and other initiatives, Spitzer is building the reputation of the attorney general as "the people's lawyer."

Spitzer is a 1981 graduate of Princeton University and a 1984 graduate of Harvard Law School, where he was an editor of the *Harvard Law Review*. Spitzer and his wife, also a Harvard Law School graduate, live in Manhattan with their three daughters.

5. Tom Vilsack

Orphaned at birth, Iowa governor Tom Vilsack has a life story that reads like an American fable. He received a bachelor's degree from Hamilton College in Clinton, New York, in 1972, and received a law degree from Albany Law School in 1975. Vilsack was elected mayor of Mount Pleasant, Iowa, in 1987, and elected to the Iowa senate in 1992. Six years later, he became Iowa's first Democratic governor in more than thirty years. He handily won a second four-year term in 2002.

In 2004 he was one of a handful of finalists to become John Kerry's running mate. Democratic National Committee press secretary Tony Welch said fifty-three-year-old Vilsack is poised for the national political stage after first attracting attention during the Iowa caucuses in January. "Nobody knew who the hell Vilsack was before the primaries," Welch told CNN. "And then his name gets bandied about, and he's a finalist. So if you were looking forward to see who is positioned for the big time eight years from now, his status goes up there."

# 10 Progressive Movers, Shakers, and Writers

1. Eric Alterman: speaking out against the free ride the mainstream media has given Bush.

   The *National Catholic Reporter* called Alterman "the most honest and incisive media critic writing today." A professor of English at Brooklyn College and the media columnist for *The Nation,* he is the author of several bestselling exposés, including *What Liberal Media? The Truth About Bias and the News* (Basic Books, 2003), and The *Book on Bush: How George W. (Mis)leads America* (Viking, 2004). His latest work, *When Presidents Lie: A History of Deception and Its Consequences* (Viking), hit bookstores in September 2004.

2. David Corn: keeping the heat on the Bush administration.

   David Corn is Washington editor of *The Nation* and writes on a host of subjects, including politics, the White House, Congress, and the national security establishment. He has broken stories on George W.

George W. Bush is out jogging one morning and notices a little boy on the corner with a box. Curious, he runs over to the child and says, "What's in the box, kid?"

The little boy says, "Kittens! They're brand-new kittens."

George W. laughs and says, "What kind of kittens are they?"

"Republicans," the child says.

"Oh, that's cute," George W. says, and he runs off.

A couple of days later George is running with his buddy Dick Cheney and he spies the same boy with his box just ahead.

George W. says to Dick, "You gotta check this out," and they both jog over to the boy with the box.

George W. says, "Look in the box, Dick, isn't that cute? Look at those little kittens. Hey, kid, tell my friend Dick what kind of kittens they are."

The boy replies, "They're Democrats."

"Whoa!" George W. says. "I came by here the other day and you said they were Republicans. What's up?"

"Well," the kid says, "their eyes are open now."

**BUSHISM:**
"I was raised in the West. The west of Texas. It's pretty close to California. In more ways than Washington, D.C., is close to California."
—In Los Angeles, as quoted by the *Los Angeles Times*,
April 8, 2000

Bush, Newt Gingrich, Oliver North, Colin Powell, Richard Gephardt, Hillary Clinton, Rush Limbaugh, the Central Intelligence Agency, the Pentagon, and other Washington players and institutions.

3. Cheryl Jacques: steering the largest gay lobbying group in the United States

Cheryl Jacques is president and executive director of the Human Rights Campaign. Her passionate commitment to civil rights and equality based on sexual orientation, gender identity, and gender expression led her to take the helm of the HRC after serving nearly a dozen years in the Massachusetts State Senate. She was first elected to her seat at the age of twenty-nine in a traditionally conservative district, proving her ability to speak to constituents across a spectrum of ideologies.

4. Charles Peters: founder of the *Washington Monthly*, one the nation's most fiery, populist media voices.

For more than three decades, Charles Peters has represented the kind of spirited and devoted crusader for the public good that the nation's founders considered a bulwark of democracy. Working with a tiny staff on a shoestring budget at his monthly magazine, Peters created a small but extraordinarily influential political journal that has changed the course of political discourse in Washington and transformed a generation of journalists.

5. John Podesta: helping create and finance a new breed of liberal think tank.

John Podesta is president and CEO of the Center for American Progress, a nonpartisan organization that promotes policies based on Americans' shared values. Podesta held several high-level advisory positions in both Clinton administrations, serving as the president's chief of staff from 1998 to 2001, and is now also a visiting professor at Georgetown University law center in Washington, D.C.

6. Ruby Sales: fortifying the infrastructure of the African American community.

    Born in Jemison, Alabama, Ruby Sales is a civil rights veteran, historian, activist, and minister. She currently serves as director of SpiritHouse, a faith-based nonprofit community development organization she launched in 2000 that "aims to achieve a nonviolent and just world through exploring the legacy of American violence, racism and sexism." Sales has also served as director of the Citizens' Complaint Center, Black Women's Voices and Images, and Women of All Colors.

7. Joshua Micah Marshall: writing one of the Internet's most intelligent websites.

    Marshall is a writer, historian, and commentator on politics, culture, and foreign affairs. His influential blog, Talking Points Memo, is among the most highly regarded in the country. His work has appeared in major newspapers including *The New York Times* and in publications including *The American Prospect,* the *Atlantic Monthly, The New Yorker,* and *Salon.*

8. Hilary O. Shelton: fighting for the NAACP in Washington.

    Hilary O. Shelton is director of the Washington bureau of the National Association for the Advancement of Colored People, the oldest, largest, and most widely recognized civil rights organization in the United States. As such, she advocates at the national level for the organization's legislative and public policy agenda. Shelton has also served in the Government Affairs Department of the College Fund/UNCF, better known as the United Negro College Fund, the nation's largest and oldest minority higher education assistance organization.

9. George Soros: funding the fight to derail the reign of the right.

Born in Budapest, Hungary, and a survivor of the Nazi occupation, billionaire investor George Soros is a philanthropist, author, and philosopher committed to putting his progressive ideals into action in his adopted home. Once dubbed "the Man Who Broke the Bank of England" for building his fortune on currency speculation, Soros has plowed his wealth into progressive causes including the Open Society Institute and the Soros foundations, giving away millions of dollars each year to programs focused on building civil society, education, media, public health, human rights, and social, legal, and economic reforms.

10. Ruy Teixeira: adding legitimacy and structure to liberal thinking.

A joint fellow at two progressive think tanks, the Center for American Progress and the Century Foundation, Teixeira is the author of five books and more than one hundred articles, as well as host of a weekly online column, Public Opinion Watch. His latest book is *The Emerging Democratic Majority* (Scribner, 2002), one of the most widely discussed and hotly debated works of 2004, which has generated praise across the political spectrum.

# 9 People Worse Than Bush (in no particular order)

1. Tomás de Torquemada

   In 1483 Tomás de Torquemada became the inquisitor-general for most of Spain. He was responsible for establishing the rules of inquisitorial procedure and creating branches of the Spanish Inquisition in various cities. He remained the leader of the Spanish Inquisition for fifteen years and is believed to be responsible for the execution of approximately two thousand Spaniards, most of whom were burned at the stake. Torquemada devised and promoted the extensive use of imaginative forms of torture, including foot roasting, the rack, slow bloodletting, and suffocation. He was made Grand Inquisitor by Pope Sixtus IV. Torquemada's hatred of Jews influenced King Ferdinand and Queen Isabella to expel all Jews who had not embraced Christianity.

2. Vlad Tepes

   Vlad the Impaler was a Romanian prince known, as his name suggests, for executing his enemies by impalement. His gruesome exploits are credited with giving rise to the Dracula legend, though Dracula's exploits appear far more sanguine. Tepes favored several forms of torture, including disemboweling and rectal and facial impalement. Vlad the Impaler tortured thousands while he ate and drank among the corpses. He impaled every person in the city of Amlas—twenty thousand men, women, and children. For his entertainment, Vlad often ordered his guards to boil, skin, blind, or strangle individuals before they were burned, hacked to death, or buried alive. He was also said to be fond of removing noses, breasts, ears, sex organs, hands, feet, and limbs.

3. Adolf Hitler

The dictator of Nazi Germany, Adolf Hitler, born on April 20, 1889, became one of history's most notorious mass murderers. His rise to power in Germany and the production of a terrifying war machine led to a global war that by its end claimed the lives of more than fifty million people. In a list of terrible people, he probably stands at the top.

4. Ivan the Terrible

Born in August 1530, in Kolomenskoye, near Moscow, Ivan Vasilyevich was the grand prince of Moscow and the first to be proclaimed tsar of Russia at the age of seventeen. Ivan soon set up a bodyguard that has been described as Russia's first secret police— the Oprichniki—as a religious brotherhood sworn to protect the tsar. Their power was absolute, and they became murderous bandits terrorizing the Russian countryside. Ivan sentenced thousands to internal exile in far-flung parts of the empire. Others were condemned to death, their families and servants often killed as well. Ivan liked to give detailed orders about the executions, using biblically inspired tortures to reconstruct the sufferings of hell. More than three thousand people lost their lives in Ivan's attack on Novgorod alone. He was said to have burned thousands of people to death in enormous frying pans and was also fond of impaling people.

5. Pol Pot

Pol Pot was born in 1925 in the Kompong Thom province of Cambodia. He was the Khmer political leader whose totalitarian regime (1975–79) imposed impossible hardships on the people of Cambodia. His radical communist government forced the mass evacuations of cities and killed or displaced millions of people, leaving a legacy of disease and starvation. Under his leadership, his government caused the deaths of at least one million people from forced labor, starvation, disease, torture, or execution.

6. Idi Amin Dada Oumee

Idi Amin, born in 1924 in Uganda, served as the military officer and president of his country from 1971 to 1979. Amin took tribalism, a long-standing problem in Uganda, to its most barbaric extreme with the state-subsidized persecution of the Acholi, Lango, and other tribes. Human rights reports indicate he was responsible for the torture and murder of one hundred thousand to three hundred thousand Ugandans, as well as, in 1972, the deportation of all Asians. Over the years, Ugandans disappeared in the thousands, their mutilated bodies washing up on the shores of Lake Victoria. Amin boasted of being a "reluctant" cannibal—human flesh, he said, was too salty. He once ordered that the decapitation of political prisoners be broadcast on TV, specifying that the victims "must wear white to make it easy to see the blood."

7. Joseph Stalin

During the quarter of a century preceding his death in 1953, the Soviet dictator Joseph Stalin, born in 1879, may have exercised greater political power than any other figure in history. In the 1930s, by his orders, millions of peasants were either killed or permitted to starve to death. Stalin brought about the deaths of more than twenty million of his own people while holding the Soviet Union in an iron grip for twenty-nine years. Stalin succeeded his hero, Vladimir Ilyich Lenin, in 1924. From then on, he induced widespread famines to enforce farm collectives and eliminated perceived enemies through massive purges.

8. Genghis Khan

The Mongol Temujin, known to history as Genghis Khan, was a warrior and ruler who, starting from obscure beginnings, brought all the nomadic tribes of Mongolia under the rule of himself and his family in a rigidly disciplined military state. Mongol hordes killed off countless people in Asia and Europe in the early 1200s. When attacking Volohoi, Khan convinced the city commander that Mongols would stop attacking if the city sent out one thousand cats and several thousand swallows. When he got them, Genghis had bits of cloth tied to their tails and set the cloth on fire. The cats and birds fled back to the city and ended up setting hundreds of fires inside the city. Then Genghis attacked and won. At another time, Mongols rounded up seventy thousand men, women, and children and shot them with arrows.

As Governor, Bush got to ceremonially act as a state trooper for a day. While operating a speed trap, Bush pulled over a Texas farmer. He lectured the farmer about his speed and the necessity of obeying laws made by his superiors, and in general threw his weight around. Finally, he got around to writing the ticket, and as he was doing so he kept swatting at some flies that were buzzing around his head.

The farmer said, "Having some problems with circle flies there, are ya, sir?"

Bush stopped writing the ticket and said, "Well, yeah, if that's what they are—I never heard of circle flies."

So the farmer said, "Well, circle flies are common on farms. See, they're called circle flies because they're almost always found circling around the back end of horses."

Bush said, "Oh," and went back to writing the ticket. After a minute he stopped and slowly said, "Hey . . . wait a minute, are you trying to call me a horse's ass?"

The farmer says, "Oh no, Governor, I have too much respect for you to even think about calling you a horse's ass."

Grinning broadly, Bush says, "Well, that's a good thing," and goes back to writing the ticket. After a long pause, the farmer says, "Hard to fool them flies though."

**BUSHISM:**
"In my judgment, when the United States says there will be serious consequences, and if there isn't serious consequences, it creates adverse consequences."

—*Meet the Press*, February 8, 2004

9. Nicolae Ceausescu

The leader of Communist Romania from 1965 until his execution in 1989, Ceausescu (born in 1918) decreed that all women must bear five children. Due to terrible food shortages, many women were unable to support their decree babies. They turned them over to state-run orphanages. More than 150,000 children were crowded into these institutions; many died of malnutrition and disease. Others ran away, becoming homeless beggars. Ceausescu also forbade testing of the nation's blood supply for AIDS. Through transfusions and shared vaccination needles, thousands of orphans contracted AIDS. Eventually Romania accounted for more than half of Europe's cases of childhood AIDS.

# 7 American Politicians More Frightening Than Bush

1. Richard Barrett

    Barrett is the founder and leader of the Nationalist Movement, a white supremacist organization based in Learned, Mississippi. Although the group has never enjoyed large-scale influence on the far right, a fact attributed in large part to Barrett's reluctance to share the spotlight, his group has been able to attract a steady number of aggressive skinheads. An attorney and tireless promoter, Barrett is best known for staging well-publicized rallies, often following legal actions that uphold the group's free speech rights. He has repeatedly drawn enormous crowds of counterprotestors, some of whom have responded violently.

2. Alan Keyes

    In the 1990s Alan Keyes became known as an outspoken champion for conservative causes via his radio talk program, *The Alan Keyes Show*. Keyes attempted to build on his notoriety with unsuccessful runs for the U.S. Senate in Maryland in 1988 and 1992 and for U.S. president in 1996 and 2000. His caustic comments in the race against Barack Obama for the U.S. Senate representing Illinois in 2004 prompted headlines all over the country. "Christ would not vote for Barack Obama," Keyes said in September 2004, "because Barack Obama has voted to behave in a way that it is inconceivable for Christ to have behaved."

Keyes also reportedly called Obama "a socialist and a liar." These antics, along with right-wing views decidedly out of step with the Illinois electorate, handed Democrats their most lopsided win in 2004.

Keyes has been counted out before, however, and he keeps coming back. He is a determined player in conservative circles, and his humiliating defeats engender sympathy among his fellow Republicans.

3. Haley Barbour

According to the Southern Poverty Law Center, the current governor of Mississippi, Haley Barbour, and several close officials continue to cultivate ties to the Council of Conservative Citizens (CCC), a white supremacist group.

Since 1998, when media reports linked then U.S. Senate Majority Leader Trent Lott to the CCC, Republicans have sought to distance themselves from the organization. The CCC has since become even more extremist, writing that blacks are "a retrograde species of humanity" and attacking "Jewish power brokers" in the media and banking industries. Governor Barbour appeared at a CCC barbecue in July 2003 and was photographed with CCC field director Bill Lord.

4. David Duke

Owing to several runs for representative office, David Duke has continued to propagandize white supremacy with a variety of fringe organizations. He is credited with pioneering the now common effort on the far right to camouflage racist ideas in hot-button issues such as affirmative action and immigration, successfully appealing to race and class resentments. He was among the first neo-Nazi and Klan leaders to discontinue the use of Nazi and Klan regalia and ritual, masking overt displays of race hatred.

Since 2001, Duke has been based in Russia and the Ukraine, where he has participated in Holocaust denial conferences and argued that Israel perpetrated the terrorist attacks on the United States on September 11, 2001. His most recent group, the European-American Unity and Rights Organization, is modeled on contemporary civil rights groups. "Just as African Americans have the NAACP and Mexican Americans have La Raza," Duke said, "European Americans now have the National Organization for European American Rights to actively defend their rights and heritage in the United States."

5. Tom Parker

Tom Parker, a Republican candidate for the Alabama Supreme Court, attended a July 2004 party in Selma commemorating the birthday of Confederate general Nathan Bedford Forrest, founder of the KKK. The funeral service resembled a rally of sorts, with Parker shaking hands, taking photographs with supporters, and handing out Confederate battle flags. There he was photographed with Leonard Wilson, a director of the white supremacist Council of Conservative Citizens, and Mike Whorton, a leader with the League of the South, a neo-secessionist hate group.

6. Patrick Johnston

A physician, vice chairman of the Ohio branch of the far-right Constitution Party, and tireless opponent of homosexuality, Johnston says gay Americans suffer from something that "merits discrimination." In fact, he says, "I support and endorse the criminalization of homosexuality, and believe the issue of whether gay Americans should be executed is a decision best left to the states."

As he told a Salon.com reporter, "If we ever had a nation sufficiently Christian" to make homosexuality illegal, imposing capital punishment for homosexuality would be a subject for "an in-house debate. There were capital crimes in the Bible, and that would be something debated."

7. Representative Tom DeLay

While carrying on a long Washington tradition of molding the nation's law to the benefit of industrial and financial interests, as House majority leader Tom DeLay has taken political corruption in the nation's capital to stellar heights. After a series of progressively more brazen actions, the House Ethics Committee finally admonished DeLay in the fall of 2004 for ethics violations, citing (among other actions) that he participated in a golf fund-raiser for energy companies just as the House was to consider energy legislation, that he offered to support the son of retiring Representative Nick Smith (R-Michigan) in exchange for Mr. Smith's vote on the Medicare pre-

A first-grade teacher is explaining to her class that she is a Republican and how nice it is that a new Republican president has taken office. She asks her students to raise their hands if they, too, are Republicans and support George Bush.

Everyone in class raises their hands except one little girl.

"Mary," says the teacher with surprise, "why didn't you raise your hand?"

"Because I'm not a Republican," says Mary.

"Well, what are you?" asks the teacher.

"I'm a Democrat and proud of it," replies the little girl.

The teacher cannot believe her ears. "My goodness, Mary, why are you a Democrat?" she asks.

"Well, my momma and papa are Democrats, so I'm a Democrat, too."

"Well," says the teacher in an annoyed tone, "that's no reason for you to be a Democrat. You don't always have to be like your parents. What if your momma was a criminal and your papa was a criminal, too, what would you be then?"

"Then," Mary said, "we'd be Republicans."

**BUSHISM:**
"Our enemies are innovative and resourceful, and so are we. They never stop thinking about new ways to harm our country and our people, and neither do we."
—Washington, D.C., August 5, 2004

scription drug bill, and that he drafted Federal Aviation Administration officials to harass Democratic Texas legislators who crossed state lines to foil his redistricting plans. For that last action, DeLay was subpoenaed to testify in a Texas civil lawsuit.

# 9 New Drinks to Get You By

Soon to appear at your local bar, courtesy of the second term:

1. Abstinence on the Beach
2. Bloody Mary Cheney
3. Tom Ridge Collins
4. Jenna Tonic
5. Old-Fashioned Family Values
6. Tequila Morning in America
7. Three Mile Island Iced Tea
8. Fuzzy Naval Intelligence
9. Banana Swift Boat

# 7 Tips for Women

*Gail Evans*

*Gail Evans is the former executive vice president of the CNN Newsgroup and is currently a visiting professor at the Georgia Tech School of Management, teaching a course entitled Gender, Race, and Ethnicity in Organizational Behavior. The bestselling author of* Play Like a Man, Win Like a Woman *(Broadway Books, 2000) and* She Wins, You Win *(Gotham Books, 2003), she lectures at corporations and women's organizations across the country.*

1. You vote with your actions every day—not just once every four years. Stay involved. Talk about the issues that matter to you when you have lunch with your friends or when you are in the carpool lane. Don't deliver diatribes (no one will listen); find easy ways to discuss how important each of us is to the political process. At lunch, talk about the kids, the shoes, and the dinner party, but save time for the issues of today's news. It will make all of you more powerful and more effective.

2. Get informed. Don't just let the passion you brought to this election fade. Become knowledgeable so that people listen to you when you speak. Read a major newspaper every day. Books like *The 9/11 Commission Report* (Norton, 2004) are actually very good reads. If you can't find the time in your schedule to read books, then rent audiobooks to listen to in the car. You will be amazed how much you learn and how quickly books on tape hook you.

3. If you supported John Kerry primarily because you support a woman's right to choose, join your local Planned Parenthood chapter. Find out whether your state is one of those on the high-risk-to-lose-the-right-to-choose list. If so, go to local meetings and meet your local representatives. What they do may be more important to your life than what the White House does.

4. Remember that this was only one election. Democrats tend to operate out of passion, Republicans out of organization. Frequently passion comes too late to make a difference. Develop a timeline. Plan for what you will do to affect the 2006 and 2008 elections. Don't start too late. Real change takes a long time. Perseverance frequently takes the day.

5. Leave your bumper stickers on the car. They will remind you and everyone else how much this election mattered.

6. Understand that one of the beauties of this democracy is the division of powers. Just because you don't agree with the White House doesn't mean that you can't have an effect on the government. Begin an e-mail campaign directed at your local congressperson or senator. Focus on the issue of most importance to you

and get your friends, church members, and relatives to join you. The politicians are your representatives, and they want to be reelected. They listen to how their constituents feel, and this affects their vote.

7. Think of yourself as one of those people who is laying the groundwork for the day when there will be a woman president. Let that thought inspire you when the going gets rough.

A Texas patrolman pulled alongside a speeding car on the highway. Glancing at the car, he was astounded to see that not only was the Texas governor, George W. Bush, behind the wheel, but that he was knitting! The patrolman must have been a Democrat, because he tried to stop the governor. But Mr. Bush was oblivious to the flashing lights and siren, so the ranger cranked down his window, turned on his bullhorn, and yelled, "Pull over!"

"No," George W. yelled back, "it's a scarf!"

**BUSHISM:**
**"I think anybody who doesn't think I'm smart enough to handle the job is underestimating."**
—*U.S. News & World Report,* April 3, 2000
(thanks to Alfred Stanley, Austin, Texas)

# 10 Retrofitted Movies for Republicans

As we all learned during their national convention, Republicans will only see movies and shows that conform to the opinions expressed in the Republican platform. Thus, all movies will have to be retitled and reedited so that we can still see them—here's the first list as handed down by the new minister of culture, Lynne Cheney.

1. *The Freedom Connection*
2. *Dances with Wolfowitz*
3. *Richard Perle Harbor*
4. *All About Adam and Eve*
5. *Men in Colorful Stripes and Solids*
6. *My Big Fat Straight Wedding*
7. *Moral Majority Report*
8. *The Fellowship of the Willing*
9. *The Twin Towers*
10. *Return of King George*

# 10 Things Parents Can Say to Their Children

*James Howe*

*James Howe is the award-winning author of more than seventy books for children, including the multimillion-selling* Bunnicula *series and* The Misfits *(Aladdin, 2001), the young-adult novel that inspired the national No Name-Calling Week project. (For information on No Name-Calling Week, go to www.nonamecallingweek.org.) Howe lives in Westchester County, New York, with his partner, Mark Davis, and his daughter, Zoey Howe.*

As a writer for children and as a parent, I'm very concerned about the effects of the Bush administration on the minds and hearts of our kids, and on their well-being now and in the future. It isn't always easy to balance the need to protect our children from anxieties about an unstable world with the need to give them truth and strength. But truth and strength are what they need, along with humor, compassion, and a keen sense of justice learned early on.

These are some things I would say (with help from Zoe and Mark):

1. I lived through Nixon; you will make it through the Bush years.
2. Bullies sometimes win, but only in the short run.
3. You too could sound like our president if you don't work hard in school.
4. Religion is about not what you say but what you do and how you treat others.
5. Everyone is entitled to equal rights. Everyone.
6. Treat the Earth and all its inhabitants with gentleness and great respect.
7. Regardless of the president's words and actions, we are global citizens and should act accordingly.
8. We are a country of many religions and beliefs—no single religion rules.
9. Who do you want for bedtime reading tonight—Al Franken, Molly Ivins, or Garrison Keillor?
10. Next time our country will get it right.

# 10 Ways to Make Money

*Russell Pearlman*

*Award-winning journalist Russell Pearlman is a senior writer at* SmartMoney. *He plans to spend the second Bush term writing a book and honing his poker skills.*

Just because you didn't vote for Bush doesn't mean that you stop living, or making a living. Why not make as much money as possible so that you can contribute that money to a candidate whom you prefer? As with any administration, there will be plenty of opportunities to make, and to lose, money. Here are some smart ways to do the former:

1. Invest in money management companies.

    Even if George Bush isn't successful in privatizing parts of Social Security, the effort will certainly put the spotlight on the program, and one fact will become abundantly clear: Social Security, in any form, will not cover your living expenses in your retirement years. Americans will need to invest in stocks, bonds, and other investments to ensure that they're not struggling in their golden years. More people will turn their money over to money management professionals, whether to asset management firms like T. Rowe Price, Eaton Vance, and Charles Schwab or to brokerage firms like Merrill Lynch or Morgan Stanley. And if Bush does get a privatizing Social Security plan through Congress, it should be called the "Keep Money Management Firms Rolling in Profits Act."

2. Roll around in coal.

He might be persona non grata at the Sierra Club; however, George Bush does recognize that if America is to continue to use coal as a source of energy, the stuff has to be cleaner. During his first term, Bush proposed to spend $2 billion over ten years to advance clean-coal technology. Expect more of the same in the second term. General Electric thinks there's money to be made in clean-coal technology, government subsidies or not. It's willing to spend hundreds of millions of dollars to develop cleaner coal-powered energy turbines. That bodes well for companies like Arch Coal and Peabody Energy, the nation's leading coal producers. I don't expect demand for their products to slack off anytime soon.

3. Go offensive on defense companies.

Bush started his term wanting to modernize the military. He finished his term vowing to increase spending for protection of troops. Expect both initiatives to be pushed in the second term. Firms like Northrop Grumman make unmanned drones to scope out terrorists, while smaller firms like Armor

Holdings provide body armor to soldiers and police officers.

4. Avoid Treasury bonds.

Despite what you might think, George Bush hasn't completely destroyed America's reputation. People and countries worldwide buy trillions of dollars in U.S. Treasury bonds because they know they are backed by the full faith and credit of the U.S. government. If an investor holds the bond until it matures, he or she will get paid back, with interest. But now is not the time to be buying U.S. debt. Interest rates are extremely low, so any Treasury bonds you buy now will not pay very much in interest. And with the nation's huge debt burden, interest rates will not stay low for long. As rates rise, the value of those Treasury bonds will fall (bond prices move in the opposite direction of interest rates). If you want to buy fixed income, look at municipal bonds, which are issued by cities and states and aren't as sensitive to interest rate movements, or corporate bonds, which will pay a higher rate than government debt.

5. Seek out investments that aren't valued in U.S. dollars.

The sputtering economy, tax cuts, and a huge jump in government spending have left the U.S. government in over a $400 billion deficit. And George Bush isn't in much of a hurry to erase that shortfall. Neither, for that matter, was Senator John Kerry. At least in the short term, this will make the dollar weaker against other currencies, such as the euro or the Japanese yen. Investing in a foreign firm or bond is essentially like buying foreign currency. The value of the foreign currency will go up as the dollar weakens, making your investment worth more.

George Bush, Sr., and George Bush, Jr., were dragging the deer they had just shot back to their truck. Another hunter approached, pulling his along, too.

"Sirs, I don't want to tell you how to do something," he said, "but I can tell you that it's much easier if you drag the deer the other way. Then the antlers won't dig into the ground."

After the third hunter left, they decided to try it. A little while later George, Jr., said to George, Sr., "You know, that guy was right. This is a lot easier!"

"Yeah," says George, Sr., "but we're getting farther from the truck."

**BUSHISM:**
"I think we agree, the past is over."
—On his meeting with John McCain,
*Dallas Morning News,* May 10, 2000

6. Take a nice vacation abroad, and do it now.

On the eve of the election, the U.S. dollar was already near an all-time low against the euro. You needed around $1.25 to buy one euro. If the U.S. dollar weakens, it will make everything outside the United States even more expensive for Americans to buy. We've already given the reason that the dollar might fall over the next several years. So if you want to ski the Alps, walk on the Great Wall of China, or scale Mount Kilimanjaro, do it earlier in Bush's second term rather than later. The vacation will take your mind off your Bush anger, and the trip most likely will be cheaper for you than it will be in 2006.

7. Set up a medical savings account.

Bush singles out egregious lawsuits as the reason health-care costs are skyrocketing. But a moratorium on all malpractice lawsuits will not cut your hospital bills in half. And Bush isn't going to demand that insurance companies or doctors cut their fees. But a relatively new plan, the medical savings account, could at least ease the pain of high medical bills for some people. Employees can sock away thousands of dollars each year, tax free, into an account that can be used to pay for medical procedures or for a high-deductible health insurance plan. The money rolls over every year, so if you don't need to tap the account one year, you can use it the next year and not have to contribute as much. These plans work best for young, healthy people.

8. Improve revenue at You, Inc.

The president is all about setting up opportunities for people to make money and not big on handing people money. That means you have to find ways to fatten your own paycheck. Some tips to focus on how to get a bigger raise: Document your on-the-job successes, promote yourself at work, and put yourself in areas of growing, not declining, businesses. And since Dubya would rather switch political parties than raise taxes, you'll keep much of that raise.

9. Put your money in an oven or a closet.

Bush is going to great lengths to promote home ownership, so you might as well capitalize by improving the value of your home. Some relatively inexpensive remodeling jobs—installing stainless steel appliances, building linen closets, or adding a cathedral ceiling—can increase the value of your house by tens of thousands of dollars.

10. Relax. Really!

A president's agenda can have a big impact on the short-term performance of an economy. But history has a tendency to smooth things out. From 1926 until 2003, the stock market returned, on average, 10.4 percent. So despite Nixon's price controls, Reagan's major deficits, and Clinton's tax increase, the U.S. economy managed to do okay over the long haul. Surely George Bush's policies can't screw up the American economy for a generation. If you don't need your money for a while, throw it in a low-cost index fund or exchange traded fund that mimics the stock market. Then channel your financial anxiety into other things.

# 6 Republican Reality TV Shows to Keep You Busy

What could be more fun than getting through the Bush years by watching Republicans take over all the reality shows as well?

1. *Republican Eye for the Liberal Guy*

    Five snappy Republicans take a hapless Democrat and clean up his act by dabbing crude oil behind his ears, teaching him how to order steak at every meal, dressing him in polyester, and putting pictures of George and Laura in every room in his house.

2. *Outsourced!*

    Six people are taken out of their jobs in Utah and flown to India, where they are placed in a large telephone answering service company and paid one hundred rupees a day.

3. *American Idle*

    Here we spend hours and hours watching eight unemployed people stand on welfare lines trying to get to the one open window.

4. *Marry a Trillionaire*

It's so like a Democrat to think that a million dollars is enough money to live on—just the cars, houses, and cosmetic surgery alone cost more than that. Here ten lucky women compete for the chance to marry a really rich eighty-seven-year old man. (Sequel: *Divorce a Trillionaire*)

5. *Trading Tax Brackets*

Two families, one in the 40 percent bracket, one in the 15 percent bracket, trade places. The hidden trick is that one of these families has actually never paid a cent in taxes—guess which one!

6. *Survivor—Manhattan*

Twelve normal Republicans are taken out of their homes in Tulsa, Oklahoma, placed in a trendy Manhattan loft with lots of abstract art, and forced to go out every night, eat raw fish, stay up until 4 A.M., and dress in really nice clothes. Who will survive? (Sequel: *Survivor—Paris*. Now that's really cruel.)

# 8 Topics to Inspire Writers

*Tracy Kidder*

*Pulitzer Prize–winning author Tracy Kidder's most recent book is* Mountains Beyond Mountains *(Random House, 2003). A contributing editor to* The Atlantic Monthly, *he lives in Massachusetts.*

If writers have any function at all, it is to write about their times. And because these are exceptional times, I hope a lot of writers will go out and find something political, juicy, and important. This second Bush term is a great opportunity for writers.

Consider:

1. Foreign policy. Take a piece of Republican legislation and examine the dire effects it has on another part of the world.
2. Taxes. There are many subjects to cover in this area, but here's one: The radical right is trying to establish a flat tax and to substitute taxes on investments with taxes on salary or use, like a value-added tax. Not all

the wealthy in this country support these policies: It's not the rich; it's just the greedy.

3. The evisceration of the Bill of Rights. Find a federal judge who's tearing it apart, or is very upset about this, and write about it.

4. Corruption. Again, there are many topics here, but consider the leaking of CIA agent Valerie Plame's identity. Or the Iraq war, and where the money we're pouring into Iraq has actually gone. Or look really closely at Halliburton or Enron, and their connections to this administration.

5. Health care. Again, there's a whole range of topics waiting to be covered—the shortage of flu vaccines, or the reasons that pharmaceutical companies aren't pursuing new antibiotics as aggressively as they should.

6. Science. Look hard at the political perversion of science, and how this administration has turned it into a policy tool. Perhaps this isn't new, but the Bush administration has crossed the line.

7. Insurance. Investigate the travesty that millions in the richest nation in the world lack basic medical insurance.

8. The economy. This administration is following a disastrous course, having taken a huge surplus and turned it into a whopping deficit—it's as if you loaned your car to a neighbor's kid and he drove it straight into a tree.

These stories may have been covered already, but often in dull ways. It's time for journalists and writers to learn that every story doesn't have two sides—more likely it has fifteen. But if you are going out and trying to be the finder of fact, at some point you have to decide what is true and what isn't. To simply recite the lies someone tells you and do nothing more with them is an abdication of a writer's responsibility. So go out and name names, and don't engage in what A. J. Liebling used to call "on the one hand this, on the other hand that" writing.

Dick Cheney gets a call from his boss, George W.

"I've got a problem," says George W.

"What's the matter?" asks Cheney.

"Well, you told me to keep busy in the Oval Office, so I got a jigsaw puzzle, but it's too hard. None of the pieces fit together and I can't find any edges."

"What's it a picture of?" asks Cheney.

"A big rooster," replies George W.

"All right," sighs Cheney, "I'll come over and have a look."

So he leaves his office and heads over to the Oval Office. George W. points at the jigsaw puzzle on his desk.

Cheney looks at the desk and then turns to W and says, "For crying out loud, Georgie, put the cornflakes back in the box."

**BUSHISM:**
**"The woman who knew that I had dyslexia—I never interviewed her."**

—Orange, California, September 15, 2000

# 7 Media Habits of Highly Effective People Who Aren't Republican

*Kurt Andersen*

*Kurt Andersen is the author of* Turn of the Century *(Random House, 1999), and Random House will publish his second novel in 2005. He writes a column for* New York *magazine, and he was previously a columnist for* The New Yorker *and* Time. *Host and cocreator of the radio show* Studio 360, *he cofounded* Spy *magazine and Inside.com, served as editor in chief of* New York, *and recently oversaw the relaunch of* Colors *magazine.*

1. Read Niall Ferguson's article "Republicans for Kerry" (www.opinionjournal.com/extra/?id=110005540).

   Recently in *The Wall Street Journal,* the non-left-wing British historian argued that Bush's reelection will be bad for Republicans (and by implication good for the rest of us) because his second term will inescapably be unsuccessful—that it will turn Bush into the American John Major and cause the Republicans to be trounced by Democrats beginning in 2008 by an American Tony Blair.

2. Avoid the left-wing opinion-silo syndrome.

   I know the right-wing base sustains itself by watching only Fox News on TV, listening only to Rush Limbaugh on the radio, and reading only Ann Coulter, but apart from being unattractive and wrong, this plainly does not win elections for the left. *Fahrenheit 9/11,* dailykos.com, and *The Nation* were very popular in the last few months before the 2004 election. If they dominate your media diet going forward, they will only make you smug and intellectually lazy. In a second Bush term, sanctimony and hysteria likely will only reinforce the left's tendency to lose and fetishize losing as a sign of virtue. Instead, for instance, read intelligent, disillusioned, hawkish anti-Bushites like Paul Berman in *Slate* and *The American Prospect,* Andrew Sullivan at andrewsullivan.com, and Mickey Kaus at kausfiles.com.

3. Maximize empirical inputs—read more facts and less pure opinion.

   Either this country goes off the rails forever into an irredeemable fantasyland of creationism, imperial misadventure, and Big Lies about the environment, or (as has always happened before) it returns to acknowledge hard facts and thus common sense. To do our parts to nudge things in the latter direction, each of us can endeavor to be the un-Bush: Be aggressively curious by reading media and books that challenge or even disturb our own assumptions, such as *The Economist, Imperial Hubris* (Brassey's, 2004), by Michael Scheuer of the CIA, and Niall Ferguson's *Colossus* (Penguin, 2004).

4. Experience schadenfreude and employ strategic reconnaissance.

Republican solidarity ended on November 3. Starting now, the right will crack and fissure as the irreconcilable contradictions between the Christian fundamentalists and the true old-school conservatives continue to fester and eventually blow. Read *The Weekly Standard* and the *National Review* both to enjoy their discomfort and anguish, and to learn how to fashion a correct response to the 2006 and 2008 election cycles.

5. Read Bob Woodward's third Bush book.

*Bush at War* (Simon & Schuster, 2002) was very kind to Bush back when Bush was waging an unambiguously correct war in Afghanistan; *Plan of Attack* (Simon & Schuster, 2004) was more skeptical about the planning of the much iffier war in Iraq but just as juicily insiderish. Presuming that Woodward does a third one, not long after his number one source, Colin Powell, leaves the administration, it will be a great, shocking read.

6. Read anything Jim Fallows writes about the administration.

If you had had only an hour or two to read journalism about Iraq policy this year, his two cover stories in the *Atlantic,* "Blind into Baghdad" and "Bush's Lost Year," were what you should have read. They are calm, authoritative, unhysterical, morally lucid, and reported up the wazoo.

7. Watch *The Daily Show with Jon Stewart* every night.

# 6 Reasons to Love Global Warming

Sometimes all we need to get by is a few encouraging words. For example, instead of being worried about global warming, why not, well, warm up to it? After all . . .

1. Your trailer in the Catskills will become oceanfront property.
2. Animal rights activists can take a break from protesting mink coats.
3. You won't have to worry about seasonal affective disorder.
4. Baseball season will last twelve months.
5. Texas will be too hot to live in and all the towns, from Dallas to Crawford, will disappear.
6. You won't have to take off your clothes to get a tan.

# 1 Internet Rule to Live By

*Tim Sanders*

*Internet executive Tim Sanders is the bestselling author of* Love Is the Killer App *(Crown, 2002). His next book is* The Likeability Factor *(Crown, 2005).*

The one rule: Google authority!

In the 1970s, during the Vietnam War protests, a standard battle cry heard around the country was "Question authority."

For the next four years you will hear Bush and Cheney make statements of so-called fact. Don't accept these facts. Google authority. See for yourself whether these statements are true.

If you use the Google search engine long enough (Google.com), you can find the answers to nearly everything. For example, you may not be able to dispute the existence of WMDs, but you can get the real story on job creation, program costs, and other topics.

When you find the facts, you can also use "word of mouse" to run your own corrections. You can send all your friends links to Web pages that dispute the administration's claims.

How far can this reach? You'd be surprised. In 2001, two business travelers were mistreated by one hotel clerk in Houston, Texas. Their reservation was canceled by a grumpy night clerk, and they were stranded in the middle of the night with no room and no apology. By dawn, they had crafted a simple PowerPoint presentation and sent it to the hotel, copying a few hundred of their friends out of their address book. They asked their friends to forward this presentation "to the world."

According to *Fast Company,* within thirty days millions of people received, opened, and read this presentation. Reporters, radio DJs, and television producers began to call parent corporation Hilton to seek interviews. They also interviewed the two businesspeople on countless programs. The hotel chain ended up donating money to a charity of choice to get these two people off the air.

When you challenge the facts in the twenty-first century, you have the power to change history. Don't let The Man get you down. If you don't believe, find the facts and run your own global correction.

# 11 Books That Will Make You Feel Better, Wiser, or More Wistful

Novels in Which the U.S. Is Even Worse Off Than Now

1. *1984,* by George Orwell

    Enjoy learning about doublethink and newspeak—hardly strangers to America in 2004—from the man who created them.

2. *It Can't Happen Here,* by Sinclair Lewis

    What if the United States was taken over by a fascist totalitarian government? Sound familiar? Lewis got there first, seventy years ago.

3. *The Plot Against America* (Houghton Mifflin, 2004), by Philip Roth

    Just published, this novel explores an alternate history in which Nazi-sympathizing Charles Lindbergh defeats Franklin Roosevelt in 1940, keeps the United States out of World War II, buddies with the Nazis, and opens reeducation camps in Kentucky.

SCIENCE FICTION BOOKS FOR WISHFUL THINKING

4. *The Door into Summer,* by Robert Heinlein

    The main character is put in suspended animation for thirty years, then wakes up, still young, with a fresh new world ready to explore. This book is for those of us who wish we could spend the next four years in a cooler somewhere.

5. *Childhood's End,* by Arthur C. Clarke

    Benevolent aliens come to Earth, overthrow all evil governments, end wars, and provide enough food and shelter for everyone. We can hope.

6. *The Mars Trilogy,* by Kim Stanley Robinson

7. *The Martian Chronicles,* by Ray Bradbury

    These two novels are about how the human race begins to colonize and transform Mars. Recommended for those who wish there was another planet to live on.

HISTORY BOOKS THAT PONDER OTHER TIMES

8. *The Wars of the Roses* (Ballantine, 1995), by Alison Weir

    If you think things are bad now, consider what it was like living in fifteenth-century England, when the Yorks and the Lancasters fought bitterly for control of the throne. Family members killed family members, thousands turned out to view public executions, and in the end, neither side really won nor lost.

9. *Pericles of Athens and the Birth of Democracy* (Free Press, 1990), by Donald Kagan

    On the other hand, if you want to read something depressing, discover that in the fifth century B.C. the Greeks established a remarkable democracy that in many ways puts ours to shame. Where is Pericles when you really need him?

SCIENCE BOOKS THAT WILL HELP YOU UNDERSTAND
YOUR RACE, IF NOT YOUR PARTY

10. *The Third Chimpanzee* (HarperCollins, 1992), by Jared Diamond

    Why in the world do humans—and Republicans—act the way they do? In part because humans are more chimpanzee than they are a distinct species; in fact, humans are closer genetically to chimps than Indian elephants are to African elephants. You'll never look at your fellow human the same way again.

11. *The Origin of Consciousness in the Breakdown of the Bicameral Mind* (Houghton Mifflin, 1990), by Julian Jaynes

    This staggeringly titled book will help you realize that human consciousness is a much newer phenomenon than has been commonly believed, and that humans, again, may not be quite as advanced as some other humans might want you to believe.

The far-right extremists have finally got it together, and they've overthrown the government. Then they start rounding up politicians to execute. A firing squad is convened, and Al Gore, Bill Clinton, and George W. Bush are all marched to a wall to be shot.

As the right-wing nuts are loading their guns, Al Gore thinks, "I've got to cause a diversion so I can get away."

He yells, "Oh, no! A tornado!" and points behind the firing squad.

As the ultraconservative fruitcakes turn around to see whether there is a tornado approaching, Al Gore jumps over the wall behind him and runs away.

The firing squad turns their attention back to the two men who are left. Clinton quickly observes how well Gore's ruse has worked and yells, "Earthquake!" As the firing squad frantically looks for a place to take cover, Clinton jumps over the wall and he, too, escapes.

The firing squad resumes its stance and proceeds to take aim at George W. Bush. Dubya, believing that he, too, can create a diversion, frantically searches his mind for another natural disaster to use. Smiling to himself, he yells, "Fire!"

**BUSHISM:**
**"There's only one person who hugs the mothers and the widows, the wives and the kids, upon the death of their loved one. Others hug but having committed the troops, I've got an additional responsibility to hug and that's me and I know what it's like."**

—Washington, D.C., December 11, 2002

# 6 Pieces of Music to Transport You to Another World

1. J.S. Bach's *Goldberg Variations*

   Nowhere can you find a safer, more rejuvenating retreat than in the sublime beauty of Bach's mathematical purity. These thirty variations on a spare, crystalline aria seem to tap into the fundamentals of a natural beauty absent and ignored by Bush and company. Particularly recommended are the masterful recordings by pianist Glenn Gould.

2. Antonín Dvořák's *New World* Symphony

   This symphony was written while Dvořák was living in a Czech colony in Iowa—long before Iowa was a battleground state. In fact, if you listened to this music, you'd think America was nothing but an assemblage of superb folk tunes and airs. Few musical pieces portray a more calm and meditative America—which is a good thing.

3. Charles Ives's *Three Places in New England*

   This piece does the reverse for American music. Likewise employing traditional melodies and themes,

Ives reworks American classics into a wild ride of dissonance, harmony, and eventually a weird sort of beauty that serves as a melodic metaphor for the dissonance in the country itself—but making it all sound more fun.

4. Aaron Copland's Third Symphony

A sprawling, heroic, and at times introspective piece, Copland's symphony reminds us that Americana can be something wonderful. The seed of this piece is *Fanfare for the Common Man,* which Copland wrote to rally Americans in World War II. We need rallying today, too.

5. Keith Jarrett's *Köln Concert*

This quintessential recording of transcendence was made during a live piano concert in Germany in 1975. Jarrett's jazzy improvisations produce melodies and rhythms that involve your mind and your heart at once—not bad for a single player on a single instrument.

6. Pink Martini's *Sympathique*

And now for something completely different: This may be the CD with the greatest potential for making you smile. With charmingly ironic renditions of classics ranging from Ravel's *Bolero* to Ary Barroso's *Brasil,* it's the best musical antidote to depression (outside of the newly released score to the animated film *The Triplets of Belleville*).

# 7 Anti-Bush Movies

These movies are for when you need someone else to say it for you.

1. *Fahrenheit 9/11* (Lions Gate Films, released 6/25/04, DVD $28.95, www.fahrenheit911.com)

   The granddaddy of all anti-Bush films, Michael Moore's documentary broke box-office records in the United States and won the best picture award at the 2004 Cannes Film Festival. Moore focuses largely on Bush's ties to the Saudi royal family and how these ties influenced the president's reaction to 9/11—including the Iraq war—but he also touches on other Bush atrocities, including the theft of the 2000 presidential election. Perhaps the most memorable clip in the film is that of Bush on the morning of September 11, staring at the children's book *The Pet Goat* for over seven minutes after his aides have told him the country is under attack.

2. *Hijacking Catastrophe: 9/11, Fear and the Selling of American Empire* (Media Education Foundation, released 6/28/04, DVD and VHS $19.95, www.hijackingcatastrophe.org)

   Running just over an hour long, this riveting documentary is more of a gut punch than *Fahrenheit 9/11*'s knee slap. The film traces the roots of neoconservatives controlling the current Bush administration back to the Reagan administration, and it places the administration's post-9/11 crusade in a larger, scarier context. The filmmakers, Jeremy Earp and Sut Jhally, interviewed a broad range of political observers, including Noam Chomsky, Norman Mailer, UN weapons inspector Scott Ritter, Daniel Ellsberg, and retired Air Force Lt. Col. Karen Kwiatkowski.

3. *Bush Family Fortunes: The Best Democracy Money Can Buy* (The Disinformation Company, released 9/28/04, $14.95 DVD, www.gregpalast.com/bff-dvd.htm)

   Originally produced by and broadcast on the BBC, this one-hour documentary follows British journalist Greg Palast as he tries to unravel the stories surrounding Bush. Though less polished than Moore, Palast is more dispassionate and goes into greater detail on such familiar themes as the stealing of the Florida vote in 2000 and the favors Bush has thrown to his friends in Big Oil and to the Saudi royal family. In addition to the documentary, the DVD also includes an extensive interview with Palast, in which he covers issues raised since the original BBC broadcast, such as the media's failures throughout the Iraq war and the potential conflicts introduced by electronic voting machines.

4. *Bush's Brain* (BeBe Films, released September 17, 2004, DVD $14.99, www.bushsbrain.com)

This eighty-minute documentary, based on the book by the same name by James Moore and Wayne Slater, focuses on the primary force behind Bush's ruthless rise to power: Karl Rove. The film traces Rove's reputation for dirty tricks all the way back to his high school days and up through campaigns of Bush opponents Ann Richards, John McCain, and Al Gore. The film pulls no punches, and it's not afraid to tie Rove to some of the lowest moments in Bush's presidency, including the leaking of CIA agent Valerie Plame's name in retribution for her husband's open opposition to the Iraq war. The film reveals that whatever Bush says or does, it most likely began as a plot in the darkness known as Karl Rove's head.

Robert Greenwald's "Un" Trilogy:
5. *Unprecedented: The 2000 Presidential Election*
6. *Uncovered: The War on Iraq*
7. *Unconstitutional: The War on Our Civil Liberties*
(Public Interest Pictures, released July 6, March 24, and October 4, 2004, respectively, DVD and VHS $9.95 each, www.publicinterestpictures.org)

Filmmaker Robert Greenwald, maker of *Outfoxed: Rupert Murdoch's War on Journalism,* presents a trilogy of documentaries about the ever-more-destructive legacy of Bush. Filling a vacuum left by mainstream media asleep at the wheel, the three films carefully document the mechanics of deception employed by the Bush machine. *Unprecedented: The 2000 Presidential Election* details the 2000 presidential election debacle in Florida, *Uncovered: The War on Iraq* unearths the administration lies that propelled America to war, and *Unconstitutional: The War on Our Civil Liberties* looks at the Patriot Act and the damage it is doing to our constitutional rights.

# 8 Games to Play with Bush's Body

First off, you'll find all these games online. You can't really play with Bush's body itself. But this is the next best thing. Is it childish to do so? Perhaps, but what's wrong with being a child now and then? It's better than being, well, you know.

1. Give Bush a Brain (www.imgag.com/product/full/ap/3067907/graphic1.swf)

   Simple concept and filled with great Bushisms, this game is a good reminder of just how far he's managed to go with the brain he has.

2. Dress 'M Up Dubya (www.oddcast.com/vhost/bush/host.php)

3. Dubya Goes to War (www.oddcast.com/bush_host.php)

   Not only can you make Bush look like a sunburnt Elton John, but you can also hear him speak lines from *The Wizard of Oz* while intoxicated, and

Before he decided to run for the presidency, George W. Bush went to his dad, George Herbert Walker Bush, for advice. Former President Bush, who is fit as a fiddle for a man in his mid-seventies, noticed that his son was a little overweight, so he advised him to go on a diet. "I want you to eat regularly for two days, then skip a day, and repeat this procedure for two weeks. The next time I see you, son, you'll have lost at least five pounds," the elder Mr. Bush said.

Well, when the younger Bush returned, he shocked his dad by having lost nearly twenty pounds.

"Why, that's amazing!" the elder Bush said. "Did you follow my instructions?"

The younger Bush nodded. "But Dad, I'll tell you, though, I thought I was going to drop dead that third day."

"From hunger?"

"No, from skipping."

**BUSHISM:**
"First, let me make it very clear, poor people aren't necessarily killers. Just because you happen to be not rich doesn't mean you're willing to kill."
—Washington, D.C., May 19, 2003

then send it to your friends. Isn't this what the internet was made for?!

4. Bush Aerobics (www.miniclip.com/bushaerobics.htm)
5. Dancing Bush (www.miniclip.com/dancingbush.htm)

    You choose the moves; you choose the setting; he just does what you tell him. If he actually exercised this much in real life, he might be a little less crabby.

6. Leader of the Free World (www.screentoys.com)

    Move the dollar sign with your mouse, and watch Bush's nose go after it! Subtle.

7. Spank Bush (www.spankbush.com)

    Kinky but cathartic. You can choose the subject area you are spanking on behalf of, as well as the spanking tool.

8. Dishonest Dubya Lying Action Figure
    (www.praesentia.us/archives/dishonestdubya.html)

    The remote control contains four outfits, lots of notable quotes, and a pretzel panic button—all this at your very fingertips.

# 7 Countries to Move to

Not everyone is going to make it through the next four years staying put. Some of you are simply going to have to find a Bush-free environment. But where?

1.  France

    *Bien sur, la France.* Land of Jefferson. Land of freedom fries and freedom toast. (Actually, freedom fries originated in Belgium, but that's not important now.)

    This country has borne the diplomatic brunt of the Bush administration's admonitions about old Europe. What better place to escape to than one full of people who will smile knowingly when you tell them you simply couldn't stay in *les États-Unis* one more minute.

    However, if you plan on staying more than three months, you'll need to apply for a visa and a *carte de séjour.* This is where the problem starts—you are going to need an employment contract as part of the application process, unless your employer handles it for you.

You can also get student visas, au pair visas, long stay visas (assuming you can get your employer to write you a letter proving your employment during your stay), artists' visas, and, of course, work visas.

As a home, France offers great food and wonderful social benefits, and the taxes are comparable to those in the United States. However, you'll need to learn French. The French don't find it cute when you mangle their language any more than we find it cute when Bush mangles ours.

If you are considering France as a new home, you should contact the local French consulate for further information and visa forms.

2. Canada

Oh Canada! How you must tire of Americans' superiority complex—and yet when things here go south, we run up north. Yes, after being the butt of way too many jokes, it's the Canadians' turn to laugh when Americans start streaming over the border, pleading for citizenship.

You can visit Canada for up to 180 days before you need a visa. After that, you will need to start showing further paperwork. You should be prepared to produce the following: a Canadian immigrant visa and Confirmation of Permanent Residence; a valid passport; a detailed list of all the personal or household items you are bringing with you and a list of items that are arriving later (if you aren't already living in Canada). You must also bring with you enough money to cover living expenses such as rent, food, clothing, and transportation for a six-month period. You may be asked to show proof of your funds.

If you fall into certain categories, you might find it easier to emigrate. Certain skilled workers, people who are willing to start businesses, and those willing to settle in small French communities should apply under special provision.

Contact the Canadian embassy for further information.

3. Spain

What a country! These doughty citizens elected a new leader even after the former government tried to manipulate a non-Iraq-related terrorist incident to scare voters. Then in a move to further separate their secular government from the Catholic majority, the newly elected leaders instituted gay marriage. Spain is also a constitutional monarchy, providing all the fun and pomp of having a king; the current ruler, Juan Carlos I, is fiercely loyal to his people and their right to govern themselves.

You are free to enter Spain for ninety days without a visa. Visas to emigrate fall into three basic categories (excluding student visas). If you have a valid job offer, you can apply for a work visa. Or perhaps you might be retiring in Spain. There is an application for a retirement visa, but you will need to prove that you possess adequate medical coverage in Spain and an income to support yourself. Then there is a visa for entry for nonlucrative purposes—you must show that you don't need to work. In addition to having medical insurance, you'll need to prove that you receive at least $75,000 annually from your investments. There's also a visa category that allows foreigners to reside in Spain to develop religious, cultural, or

One day old Dick Cheney, feeling sorry for the kidding his boss gets, said, "Oh, they're only jokes. There are a lot of stupid people out there. Here, I'll prove it to you."

Cheney took him outside and hailed a taxi.

"Please take me to 29 Nickel Street to see if I'm home," said Cheney.

Without saying a word, the cabdriver drove them to Nickel Street, and when they finally got out, Cheney looked at George W. and said, "See! That guy was really stupid."

"No kidding," replied George W. "There was a pay phone just around the corner. You could have called instead."

**BUSHISM:**
"Security is the essential roadblock to achieving the road map to peace."

—Washington, D.C., July 25, 2003

scientific activities, exempting you from needing permission to work, but that route seems a little complicated.

4. Costa Rica

From the U.S. State Department: "Costa Rica joined the Coalition for the Immediate Disarmament of Iraq [Willing], despite significant domestic opposition . . ." That said, what's important is this domestic opposition—most Costa Ricans feel the same way we do about the war in Iraq, despite our governments' kowtowing to each other.

Other than that, why Costa Rica? It's one of the most beautiful countries in the world, it isn't far from your relatives in America, it has a government that sponsors ecotourism and conservation, and the cost of living is low.

You may enter Costa Rica for ninety days; after that, you will need to seek an extension based on special circumstances, usually involving an academic, medical, or employment situation. An application for residency can sometimes be completed while you are in the country if you are a retiree (of which there are many, including quite a few Americans).

An application for a work visa requires that you provide your diplomas and credentials as proof of your ability to practice your profession. Note that since November 2003 you must bring your passport with you; prior to that, U.S. citizens were able to enter the country with a picture ID and a birth certificate.

5. New Zealand

While New Zealand was a part of Operation Enduring Freedom, it has also participated in the Provincial Reconstruction Team in Afghanistan.

Thankfully, it was not among the Coalition of the Willing.

Unlike most countries, nearly all of New Zealand is ravishingly beautiful. The people are friendly, the food is fresh, and although neighboring Australia has taken a sharp turn to the right, progressives are welcome here.

As in most countries, you may stay in New Zealand for ninety days without a visa. If you want to stay longer you will need to apply for an extension of your visitor's permit, which you can do online. If you want to emigrate to New Zealand, the standard options apply.

However, note that you may also apply for a visa (or New Zealanders may sponsor you) in order to join your family, including dependent children, siblings, and/or your partner. "Partner" in New Zealand is indeed the all-inclusive term that it isn't in the United States; a marriage certificate is not required (although you will have to provide evidence that your partnership is genuine and stable).

6. Iceland

Iceland is cool in so many ways. Besides being the home of the trendsetting, poultry-dress-wearing singer Björk, the northern Atlantic island is moving toward a completely petroleum-free energy policy. The whole country is heated geothermally from all the volcanic activity underground, and the electricity is hydroelectrically produced.

And it's not really covered in ice—that's Greenland.

Iceland benefits greatly from the Gulf Stream, keeping winter somewhat manageable for someone who is used to a Northeast winter in the United States. The average temperature is thirty degrees in winter, with very little sunlight. Summer is a bit humid and cool, averaging fifty-two degrees, but the sun seems to shine constantly. The country is about the size of Virginia, and the majority of the population lives on the coast in the southwest.

Three-month stays do not require a visa, but anything longer will require a visa for residency, study, or work.

7. Pitcairn Island

This tiny southern Pacific island is where the mutineers from the H.M.S. *Bounty* fled to escape Captain Bligh in 1789. Thus, it's a place with a tradition of fleeing from injustice. Today about fifty people live here, most direct descendants of the mutineers.

It's not easy to live on Pitcairn: Mail service takes approximately three months, and for medical attention Pitcairners must wait for a ship to transport them to New Zealand, several thousand miles to the west. Nor is there much to do; Great Britain has until now subsidized the island, but it is uncertain whether it will continue to underwrite the expenses of its tiny but costly colony.

It's not easy to emigrate here, either. No ninety-day visa. You have to apply to be allowed on the island and then a local council must approve the application. After that, you have to reapply every six months. Once you hit four years, the governor can choose to give you permanent residency status.

Still, if you want to make a statement, moving to Pitcairn is about as strong a statement as you can make.

# 8 Excuses for Being Late to Work

No matter how bummed out you are, you can at least try to use the reelection as an excuse to slack off at work. That's the time-honored tradition for all Americans.

1. Your house is now being used as Dick Cheney's Undisclosed Location.
2. They finally announced a flu lottery at your local mall.
3. You had to renew your expired Cipro prescription again.
4. The line to register for the draft was longer than you expected.
5. You had to change your outfit to match this morning's new terrorist alert color.
6. You are being held as an enemy combatant and won't be released for six years.
7. You were still waiting in line to vote.
8. They discovered weapons of mass destruction in your youngest child's lunch box.

(Actually, none of this matters, because the truth is, you were laid off six months ago.)

# 13 Ways to Pass as a Republican

Certainly one time-honored tradition for dealing with the recent election is to flip-flop. Did I say I was a Democrat? Oh, my no, I'm a Republican. The only problem here is that you're going to have to change some of your habits, because Republicans will sniff out your hidden liberal ways if you're not careful. Thus, you must:

1. Forget about spending Sunday morning reading *The New York Times* and join a church (but never actually attend—instead, you sneak off to play golf).
2. Get rid of all your natural-fiber fabrics and dress in red polyester. The more it pills, the better.
3. Ditch that fuel-efficient Toyota Prius and buy a Hummer (explaining, of course, that you really wanted a more manly car but they wouldn't let you drive a tank home).
4. Throw out all those bleeding heart ribbons you've got on your jacket and get yourself a great big rhinestone American flag lapel pin.

5. Burn your Barbra Streisand records and replace them with Jessica Simpson's.

6. As a good Republican, you can no longer dance well. If you are dragged up to the dance floor, sweat nervously and sway wildly out of rhythm.

7. Stop ordering all those girly organic foods and ingest nothing but steroid-laden, hormone-infested red meat.

8. Stop eating any real food at all and start stocking up on edible petroleum products.

9. Men: Rather than having a secret crush on Katie Couric, tell everyone about the time you and Ann Coulter made out under the table at a raucous Nebraska Chamber of Commerce meeting. Women: You no longer think George Stephanopoulos is cute; you now swoon over hunky Karl Rove.

10. Stop worrying about the rights of any living adult because you now realize that all human rights begin with conception and end at birth.

11. Tune out Letterman; tune in to Leno.

12. Jon Stewart: no longer the funniest man alive; now Tucker Carlson's butt boy.

13. Instead of praising that new senator from Illinois, Barack Obama, whine about how voter fraud must have kept his rival, Alan Keyes, from office.

Four eminent doctors were having cocktails in the bar of the Beijing Hilton after attending an international medical conference.

The British doctor says, "Medicine in my country is so advanced that we can take a kidney out of one man and put it in another and have him looking for work in six weeks."

The German doctor says, "That's nothing, we can take a lung out of one person, put it another, and have him looking for work in four weeks."

The Russian doctor says, "In my country medicine is so advanced we can take half the heart out of one person and put it in another and have them both back looking for work in two weeks."

The American doctor, not to be outdone, says, "You guys are way behind. We just took a man with no brain out of Texas, put him in the White House, and now half the country is looking for work, and the other half is preparing for war."

**BUSHISM:**
**"I'm honored to shake the hand of a brave Iraqi citizen who had his hand cut off by Saddam Hussein."**
—Washington, D.C., May 25, 2004

# 5 Great Golf Courses

*John Paul Newport*

*John Paul Newport has been writing about golf for a decade. He is executive editor at a major golf magazine and the author of* The Fine Green Line: My Year of Adventure on the Pro-Golf Mini-Tours *(Broadway Books, 2000).*

For the many people who simply don't *get* golf, one of the sport's seeming drawbacks is the time required to play a round. Four hours is considered a fast round at many courses, and that doesn't include the time it takes to get there, warm up beforehand, and exchange boozy stories about the round afterward. For bona fide golf addicts, however, the game's time-consuming character is at the heart of its appeal. Time spent on the golf course is time spent beyond the reach of cell phones, official duties, and domestic responsibility. The game is a refuge, kind of willful oblivion to the rest of life. And in this sense, for those so inclined, golf is an excellent way to weather the second Bush administration. The only significant downside is the disproportionate number of Republicans involved with golf, but for each of the following five golf destinations, strategies are suggested for dealing even with this.

1. Bandon Dunes, Oregon (www.bandondunes.com)

   Miles and miles from nowhere, gorgeously situated in the primal dunes of Oregon's rugged and largely undeveloped Pacific coastline, this relatively new resort is all golf and nothing but golf. Many already consider the two courses here to be the best tandem of courses anywhere in the world, eclipsing even Pebble Beach and Cypress Point in California and the Old and New courses at St. Andrews, Scotland. The lodge features suites of rooms built specifically to accommodate traveling foursomes, so it's possible for bands of Democratic brothers and sisters to insulate themselves politically from whomever else may be present. The prices at Bandon, considering the quality of the facilities, are surprisingly democratic, and you may also find political sympathy among the caddies, many of whom are formerly unemployed lumberjacks.

2. Ballybunion, Ireland (www.ballybuniongolfclub.ie)

   This legendary, mystical course on the southwest coast of Ireland is about as far removed from uptight Republican country club golf as it's possible to be. With heart-swelling views of the sea from every rise and idiosyncratic greens nestled deep in dune hollows that were formerly occupied by leprechauns, Ballybunion will slap a big old grin on your face that won't go away for at least a week after you leave. Your Irish hosts, who, despite everything, still love Americans, will help restore your faith in America's international future. And even more heartening to exiled Democrats is the world's only statue of Bill Clinton, smack in the middle of tiny Ballybunion town. The citizens there erected the statue a few years ago out of gratitude to Clinton for services to Ireland—and also for his having played at Ballybunion during his presidency.

3. Cape Cod, Massachusetts (Olde Barnstable Fairgrounds Golf Course: www.obfgolf.com; Pinehills Golf Club: www.pinehillsgolf.com)

For the general public, golf opportunities are skimpy on John Kerry's vacation-home island of Nantucket, but Massachusetts is downright liberal when it comes to open-access courses on nearby Cape Cod. The Olde Barnstable Fairgrounds Golf Course, built in 1992 with municipal funds, is one of the best. Not far away on the mainland, just a stone's throw from that most symbolic of New England places, Plymouth Rock, are two other superb courses at Pinehills, one by Rees Jones and one by Jack Nicklaus. For recovering Democrats, the best thing about playing golf in Massachusetts is that you can talk politics freely. Here it's the Republicans who have to be circumspect.

4. Whistler Mountain, British Columbia, Canada (www.whistler.com)

If fleeing to Canada after the November election appeals to your sixties-bred sensibility, consider meeting up with fellow travelers at Whistler Mountain. Less than a two-hour drive from Vancouver, Whistler is Canada's number-one-ranked ski resort. But in the summer it transforms itself into a top-notch golf destination. With four elite courses (by Robert Trent Jones, Jr., Arnold Palmer, Jack Nicklaus, and Robert

Cupp) and lots else to do in the surrounding Rocky Mountains, Whistler is an alpine paradise—and almost Swiss-like in its neutrality.

5. Sea Island, Georgia (www.seaisland.com)

Sea Island is a conservative place—traditional, family-oriented, wealthy, and Southern—but that's the point. For dispossessed Democrats, playing golf here is missionary work. Connected to the mainland via a causeway about an hour north of Jacksonville, Florida, Sea Island is a private resort and residential enclave of the highest order. Rooms at the Lodge at Sea Island start at $500 a night in season and include the services of a butler. But being a guest grants you access to three of the finest golf courses in the South and an array of well-run, highly secure recreational activities for the kids. In such opulent circumstances— behind the barricades, so to speak—the political defenses of even the most hard-core Bushies will be down. The revolution starts here! The only danger, after a few days in luxurious residence at the Lodge, is going native.

# 13 Steps to Protect Your Body

*Mark Liponis*

*Mark Liponis, M.D., is the corporate medical director of Canyon Ranch, the world's leading health resort, and the co-author of the bestselling book* Ultraprevention *(Simon & Schuster, 2003).*

There's never any reason to let your body suffer. No matter how much you dislike the election results, you must take care of yourself, even when you feel more like panicking than exercising. Think of it this way: Now more than ever, you need to maintain your good health (and not just because the cost of medical care is only going to keep rising). If you're going to fight back, you'll need as much strength as possible to do it.

1. Fight panic. When the fight-or-flight mechanism springs into action, combat it by breathing calmly, relaxing your belly, and making sure that it moves out when you breathe in (this slows down your breathing rate). You'll also need to stretch a little—your shoul-

ders, arms, and back. Try as many stretches as you know.

2. No bingeing. When bad things happen, people do bad things to their body—they drink alcohol, eat cookies, stuff chocolate in their mouths. Don't let the election destroy your health. Instead, if you need to feed, try decaffeinated tea, which stills the urge to put something bad in your mouth.

3. Give up coffee. Caffeine fuels the fires of panic. If you don't, at least go decaf, or it will be a long four years.

4. Try saying a mantra to help you relax. A friend uses this one: "Only 1,461 days left."

5. Take stress vitamins. A good B-complex, taken along with your normal multivitamin, may be best. B's are your stress vitamins—when the body is under stress, it uses them up quickly and they must be replenished.

6. Monitor your blood pressure. Fear, anxiety, and unhappiness make it rise. Buy a home monitor to make sure your blood pressure doesn't go through the roof. And take extra calcium, magnesium, and potassium—these keep the blood pressure down. You can buy the first two in supplement form; the third you will get from orange juice, bananas, and vegetables.

7. Consider relaxation therapy. Get a massage; soak in a hot tub; take up yoga; keep a candle lit for 1,461 days.

8. Do aerobic exercise two to three times a week. Perhaps the best practice is to work out those inner frustrations on a punching bag. Stick a picture of Bush on it if you wish.

9. For men: Bank your own sperm. If environmental rules are weakened further, making the water dirtier and the air more polluted, the quality of your sperm

The GOP National Committee announced today that it was changing the Republican emblem from an elephant to a condom. The committee stated that it feels a condom more clearly reflects the party's true political stance. A condom stands up to inflation, halts production, destroys the next generation, protects a bunch of pricks, and gives one a sense of security and safety while screwing others.

BUSHISM:
"Too many good docs are getting out of the business. Too many ob-gyns aren't able to practice their love with women all across the country."
—Poplar Bluff, Missouri, September 6, 2004

will diminish. With the limits on arsenic and mercury being rolled back already, you'll need to protect those little babies.

10. Bank your own blood. Continued cutbacks in public health and Medicare will mean the blood supply will suffer. So if you're having elective surgery for something like a hip replacement, it's a good idea to have some of your blood on hand. Go to your favorite hospital and tell them you want to donate blood for yourself. They'll take your blood and store it for you.

11. Safeguard your house and family. Again, because of weakening environmental regulations, buy a reverse-osmosis water filter, as well as a HEPA filter to remove pollution particles and industrial waste from the air. This is most important in your bedroom. And watch out for beef and chicken—less environmental regulation here means that toxins in meat will increase. Consider organic vegetables, or, if you want to continue your carnivorous habits, organic free range meats.

12. Grow your own. Years ago, it was a sign of wealth when people moved from living off the land to a home in a city. Now, those who can afford it are going back to the land. What better way to make sure your food is safe than to know where it's been from start to finish. Just be organic, creative, and hungry. (And you don't have to be rich. You can grow herbs in a window box, or tomatoes on a rooftop. Use your imagination, and you can have food growing out of almost anything.)

13. Learn a new joke every day. You have to keep laughing.

# 4 Treatments to Make Your Body Feel Better

Desperate situations require desperate remedies. Getting a facial to combat your stress/anger/despondency is like putting a Band-Aid on a burst aorta. And yet, sometimes it really seems to work. Here are a few ideas for trying to get some control back into your life through alternative body treatments.

1. Isolation/flotation tank

    It's bigger than a bread box, but it's more or less shaped like one. An isolation tank is about the size of a twin bed and is filled with ten inches of water in which has been dissolved eight hundred pounds of Epsom salts. Inside, the air is as warm as the water, which is as warm as your skin. As you stretch out in the water, you will bob to the surface like a cork. You will lose the ability to distinguish water from air, and your mind will empty and clean itself out. No more problems—at least while you are floating.

    Many people worry that they'll feel claustrophobic in the tank. Not so. The tank has a door on the end that you can leave open or not, depending on your comfort level, as well as a filtration system that quietly introduces fresh air into the tank from the room. With the door shut, you are in complete darkness, and instead of feeling the tank walls around you, you may feel you are floating in infinity.

Finding one of these things is not easy. In vogue twenty-five years ago, they're less common now. Samadhi Tank Company (www.samadhitank.com) makes models for office and home use. You might also try searching the Internet under "flotation tank" or "isolation tank" and your geographic area.

2. Watsu

If lying in Epsom salts inside a box isn't your idea of heaven, perhaps you should consider watsu. Watsu is basically a floating massage.

Peaceful and serene, you lie in a warm pool with the help of a therapist while being massaged and gently led through the water. You might notice stretching, flexing, and some aspects of a deeper massage during your session. But much like the flotation tank, the effect of the water and buoyancy will let your mind travel. As your body floats freely, so will your mind.

Watsu was developed at Harbin Hot Springs in 1980 by Harold Dull when he combined elements of Zen shiatsu and warm water pools, and there are now practitioners throughout most of the United States. The facility must have a warm-water pool approximately four feet deep and large enough in area to move someone freely through the water. Watsu is well worth the effort if you can find a place that offers it.

3. Himalyan body rejuvenation treatment

Starting out as a familiar spa experience, this treatment usually involves exfoliation and friction massage to prepare the body for relaxation and then an aromatherapy steam treatment. What sends this procedure into the stratosphere is when the attendants wheel up a large container of a "plant-based" concentrate and then open the stopper on the container's bottom as it is directed in a stream onto your forehead, right between your eyebrows and running off the top of your head.

Although this might sound like a form of water torture employed at Abu Ghraib, at the end of the treatment, you'll find that you are so relaxed you'll have trouble forming complete sentences—and we all know people who do that. This treatment can be found at some Aveda spas and other selected facilities.

4. Colon hydrotherapy

Consider everything that has entered your colon during the past four years. It's a good idea to give the whole thing a good flushing before it really gets out of hand. (Yes, if only we could administer a colonic to the government, as well.)

During a colonic, you'll be irrigated with gallons of water to make sure everything inside is squeaky clean. The process is more or less what you can imagine, but most colon hydrotherapists use a closed system, which eliminates any embarrassment for the client.

The physical results are obvious, but the mental results are just as effective. You'll have eradicated four years of waste, leaving yourself open and pure.

# 5 Lovable Dog Breeds to Adopt

*The Winnipeg Humane Society*

*The Winnipeg Humane Society is the primary animal welfare organiza-tion in Manitoba. One of the world's most progressive humane societies, it has led the way in developing proactive programs to address the pet over-population problem and to promote the humane treatment of all animals. They are currently raising funds for a much needed new home to facilitate the expansion of their community programs. For more information, and to help, check their website at www.winnipeghumanesociety.ca.*

The one thing you know for sure: Your dog didn't vote for Bush. You can't blame him. In fact, your dog may be one of your best resources for unconditional love in a time of fear and anxiety. So try a little canine therapy—rub your face in your dog's fur and tell him how happy you are that he exists.

If you don't have a dog, now may be the best time to get one, or two. You need a friend. Here are five of the most lovable breeds.

1. Golden retriever

   These classic happy, friendly, and outgoing canines will make you feel like God's gift to the world every time you walk through the door. They are beautiful to behold, and their long, silky coats give you a warm and fuzzy feeling every time you touch them. They aren't known for aggression, so don't count on them to bark when people come to the door, but their size and energetic greeting may still intimidate. These dogs need a lot of activity, and just as the name says, they are exceptional at retrieving, particularly in the water. Goldens are long-lived large dogs, which makes it likely that your good friend will be with you for a long time compared to other large dogs. This breed is known for being great with kids, so consider one seriously if you have a young family.

2. Saint Bernard

   These versatile giants traditionally have been used for guarding, herding, and even drafting. Their tremendous loyalty and dedication make them ideal family pets. You know that if you ever get stranded in the snow, your Saint Bernard will be there to warm you up with a flask of brandy around his neck, just like his forebears did for all those mountaineers in the Alps. They also make wonderful indoor space heaters. Most often they are tranquil, gentle, and sociable dogs who are very devoted to their families and usually adore children. They're big guys though, weighing up to 225 pounds, so you need lots of space to share your home with a Saint Bernard. Their size will certainly intimidate any unwanted visitors until they find out what big, soft cuddlers they really are.

3. Collie

Alert watchdogs, collies are quick to detect nearby changes and are very protective of their families. Loyal and reliable, they make great companions. Just like Lassie, they will always come to the rescue if the Bush administration makes you think terrorists are around the corner. Their aristocratic bearing is beautiful and dignified, but don't let that fool you. They still want to be active and burn off steam every day. Their descendants, Scottish herding dogs, spent their days rounding up sheep, so these modern-day Lassies need their daily workout as well. Although they can be heroic, they can also be a little sensitive and timid, so don't let their dignified demeanor make you think they don't want a lot of loving—they do.

4. Shih tzu

These little bundles of fur are the ultimate lovable and cuddly lapdogs. Just what you need to remind you of one of the most important things in life: snuggling. They are the product of liaisons between the Lhasa apso of Tibet and the Pekinese from China, but they are much more outgoing than their Asian cousins. Their beautiful fur does need daily attention, and they require a little ponytail to keep their hair out of their eyes, but don't let their doll-like perfection mislead you. Although sweet and playful, they make great watchdogs who will bark to announce the arrival of wanted or unwanted guests. Remember though, once guests see them, they probably won't find them threatening.

5. Humane Society specials

These mixed-breed dogs are the perfect antidote to a right-wing, ultraconservative agenda. Humane

Society specials are all-inclusive, fascinating feats of nature combining so many different characteristics, and they are so grateful to be getting a second chance in life with you. These dogs combine the best characteristics of so many breeds, and you can pick them in almost any size, shape, or color, furry or not. They've already seen some of life's hard knocks, so when they go home with you, they're so appreciative of almost everything (except maybe the rules of the house). They'll quickly worm their way into your heart and before you know it, you'll wonder how you lived without them. You can pick your Humane Society special to match your particular lifestyle, whether its couch potato or marathon runner; there's bound to be one just right for you. (The special is also known as a mutt.)

Note: Cats are great, too. But their specific breeds aren't as distinctive as those of dogs; with the exception of a few breeds, such as Maine coon, Siamese, and Abyssinian, most people don't care about the pedigree. All they want is a loving, sweet animal. That's what a great cat will do for you—love you like you've never been loved before. The best way to find a cat is to go to the nearby pound or shelter and rescue one. Cats will make you think nothing is wrong in the world as they carelessly and happily romp and lounge in their dominion, also known as your home.

# 2 Mental Health Strategies

1. Get hypnotized.

   What if you could have yourself put under a four-year-long hypnotic spell that would make you think Kerry actually won the election? Is that even an option?

   "I think it's possible," says David R. Barron, a certified hypnotist based in San Jose, California. "I've known hypnotists who were able to convince smokers that they had never smoked," he says. The only problem is that the end result is usually a lot of fighting among people who remember things a little differently.

   Barron says one man couldn't see a cigarette in his hands in a snapshot his friends showed him. "For most people reality is much too firm for that to last very long, and if in fact someone wants to believe that Kerry is the president, it might also help to live in a basement with no access to media or social contact."

   Can you change someone's political affiliations with hypnotism? Get that Republican friend or foe to jump teams? "Human beings are very dynamic," says Barron. "There is a possibility, though slim, of changing someone's beliefs." Generally, however, he says it won't be long until they convert back.

Talk to a hypnotist prior to going under, to see how comfortable you feel with him or her. Many hypnotists will even provide a free consultation.

For more information, visit Barron's website at www.changework.com, or check your yellow pages to find a hypnotist in your area.

2. Join a support group.

Ellie Amel, a clinical social worker in New York City, suggests that support groups can be the best way to help people deal with Bush. "Spend time with other people who feel the same way you do about the Bush presidency; you can even make plans for where to go from here that will make you feel more empowered," she recommends.

Several studies have proven the efficacy of support groups in diminishing the likelihood of depression, anxiety, and other mental health problems—more commonly associated with illness, not postelection blues. Yet just like other things that we feel powerless over and cannot change—at least in this case until the next election—we just need to live through it, says Amel. "Take it one day at a time."

If you have trouble finding folks in your area who share your concerns, don't fret. There are many online newsgroups, chat rooms, and bulletin boards where people can sound off about their feelings and ideas for the future. To find support groups and links to websites on various topics, visit www.mentalhelp.net/selfhelp.

# 6 Reflections on Depression

*Andrew Solomon*

*Andrew Solomon is the author of* The Noonday Demon: An Atlas of Depression *(Scribner, 2001), which won a National Book Award, was a finalist for a Pulitzer Prize, and has been published in twenty-two languages. He is currently writing a book on families of traumatic children—kids who are deaf, gay, autistic, terminally ill, and so on. To keep himself free of despair, he is also writing a comic novel.*

1. There has been hot debate in recent years about whether depression is organic and the result of bad brain chemistry or is circumstantial and the result of events. The received wisdom seems to be that you have an organic vulnerability that is triggered by bad events. If you're very vulnerable, a slight event will put you over the edge. If you're relatively invulnerable, it takes a much more major event. The reelection of George Bush is a major event. Beware.
2. You will probably feel some of these symptoms: lack of vitality, despair, sleeplessness and anxiety, sleepi-

ness and a sense that life is purposeless, a tendency to eat too much to calm down, a feeling that life is sickening and so you can't eat, diminished interest in sex, self-abnegation, impulses to suicide, listlessness, and the feeling that the horror of life is its only reality.

3. You should do all the usual things that you would do for a depression: go on medication, go to therapy, get electroconvulsive treatments, regulate your sleep and eating, put yourself on a schedule, avoid being alone, try eye movement desensitization and reprocessing, pray, focus on improving your knitting skills, and persuade yourself that suffering is meaningful and profound.

4. It is worth noting that recent research has shown that depressed people often have a more accurate view of life than their nondepressed counterparts. The same research has shown that having an accurate view of life is not an advantage. The best strategy is denial.

5. Practice believing that the election didn't really signify anything, that Bush is a smart and kind man, that the Democrats are still really running the show, that it's just four years and not much can go wrong in four years, that ultimately the presidency is not what matters, and that you have the power to make things better by just being you.

6. Lie to yourself. It may make it easier to tolerate all the lying to you that will be a hallmark of this administration.

# 5 Excellent Antidepressants

Bush has you feeling depressed. Really depressed. You're not alone. More than eighteen million Americans suffer from depression—clinical depression. Clinical depression doesn't discriminate on the basis of race, class, religion, or political party—it can strike anyone, including Republican presidents Calvin Coolidge and Richard Nixon.

When depressed, most people turn to psychiatric therapy or pills such as Celexa, Prozac, and Zoloft. These work for some; not for others. Here are five more reliable alternatives:

1. Levitra (for men)

    Yes, it's still a pill, but what a pill! Instead of taking six weeks like Prozac, Levitra goes to work in minutes. It makes you feel really good, and it makes someone else feel less depressed, too. Recommended dosage: as often as needed.

2. Pasta

    In the 1960s no one ate pasta because it was bad

for you. In the 1980s everyone ate pasta because it was good for you. Now it's bad for you again. The fact is, pasta tastes so great that it makes you feel good in minutes, and, anyway, soon nutritionists will change their minds again and declare that it's healthy. Think of all the excellent pasta you'll have missed in the meantime. Recommended dosage: at least three times a week.

3. Dove dark chocolate bar

Nutritionists, not John Kerry, are the ultimate flip-floppers. After warning us off chocolate for years, now they're telling us that dark chocolate has some of the same cancer-fighting phytochemicals as green tea, grapes, and blueberries. And it releases endorphins, like Prozac. Dove makes the best of these handy over-the-counter antidepressants. Recommended dosage: four times a week.

4. A pedicure

Here's a secret women have known for years, but they won't tell men. A pedicure isn't really about having your toes painted pink. It's a wonderfully soothing foot treatment that not only makes your feet look great, but makes them feel great, too. And if your feet feel great . . . Recommended dosage: as often as necessary.

5. BBC-TV

*Absolutely Fabulous. Coupling. The Office. Monty Python.* Okay, Tony Blair is Bush's lapdog. But at least the rest of the British are funny enough to transport you out of your political depression. Recommended dosage: several hours a day.

Pappy Bush, his son Jeb, and his other son Dubya were in a bar enjoying a few quiet drinks one night when they decided to get in on the weekly raffle.

They bought five $1 tickets each. The following week, when the raffle was drawn, they each won a prize.

Pappy Bush won the first prize—a whole year's supply of gourmet spaghetti sauce.

Son Jeb was the winner of the second prize—six month's supply of extra-long gourmet spaghetti.

Dubya won the sixth prize—a toilet brush.

When they gathered in the same bar a week later, Pappy asked the others how they were enjoying their prizes.

"Great," said Jeb. "I love spaghetti."

"So do I," said Pappy. "And how's the toilet brush, Dubya?"

"Not so good," Dubya said. "I reckon I'll go back to paper . . ."

BUSHISM:
"Free societies are hopeful societies. And free societies will be allies against these hateful few who have no conscience, who kill at the whim of a hat."
—Washington, D.C., September 17, 2004

# 7 Modern Virtues to Live By

*Anita L. Allen*

*A graduate of Harvard Law School, Anita L. Allen is the Henry R. Sil-verman Professor of Law and a professor of philosophy at the University of Pennsylvania. She is the author of* The New Ethics: A Tour of the 21st Century Moral Landscape *(Miramax, 2004) and several books about privacy and personal accountability.*

Your side lost. You are disappointed, angry, and worried about the future. But keep two things in mind. First: Political defeat is not a reason for questioning your fundamental values. They won, but you could be right. So rededicate yourself to what you know in your heart are the requirements of personal integrity, humane care, and global justice. Second: Times of disappointment like these are a test of character. You will do yourself proud to cope well with a Republican in the White House by practicing modern versions of seven ancient virtues:

1. Patience

    Take time with the slow, partisan political process that impedes necessary change.

2. Generosity

    Give abundantly to others, because ours is a nation whose lawmakers often favor the rich at the expense of the poor, sick, and elderly.

3. Temperance

    Be circumspect in the use of deadly military force to preempt aggression against your country and allies.

4. Justice

    Be swift, fair, and humane in the punishment of criminal offenders; give all captives and detainees the due process required by the just rule of law.

5. Tolerance

    Respect those whose point of view, race, or religion is different from your own.

6. Loyalty

    Consistently tend caring, cooperative relationships.

7. Honesty

    Tell the truth and demand it from your leaders.

# 1 Way to Tell If Bush Is Lying

Nick Morgan, Ph.D., one of the nation's foremost speech coaches, is an expert on body language; his most recent book is *Working the Room* (Harvard Business School Press, 2002).

Morgan says there are two ways to tell whether someone is lying: the easy way and hard way. The easy way happens when you know people well enough to see the lie behind the emotion leak out through body language, such as a physical twitch or a quick facial expression.

The hard way is to read what Morgan calls microexpressions on the faces of people you don't know. If you watch these people closely, you will notice split-second changes in expression take place as they lie.

Morgan has studied Bush since watching him give the State of the Union address before the Iraq war. He says that when Bush lies, his eyes dart quickly from side to side. "The moment I saw this was when he said that he wanted peace with Iraq and that he would seek out every possible avenue for peace. I knew then that the war was a done deal.

"Watch Bush's eyes dart, and you will be able to see him lie."

Note: Morgan says that Condoleezza Rice is a terrible liar. "It's written all over her face. When she lies, her face goes rigid—she tries to conceal the fact that she is lying by freezing. It's so obvious that anyone could make a lot of money playing in a high-stakes poker game with her."

# 9 Prayers to Get You Through the Night

*Timothy Dobbins*

*Timothy Dobbins is an Episcopal priest, a conflict negotiator, and the president of culturalarchitects.com, a consulting firm that helps people and organizations make a difference. The author of* Business Companion: French *(Random House, 2003), he received his master's of divinity degree from the Episcopal Seminary in Alexandria, Virginia, and studied at St. George's College, Jerusalem and at the C. G. Jung Institute in Zurich. He is both a fellow of and guest lecturer at the Wharton School.*

Religion, especially mixed with politics, can be a lethal combination. But praying is spiritual. It is not owned by any specific religion or its representatives. To pray is to listen to the still, small voice residing in each one of us.

The following prayers come from various spiritual traditions and many diverse cultures, and are meant to spark your spiritual imagination and leave you with a sense of hope for our future. In the long, dark nights ahead, you will find that a good prayer can be one of your best companions.

How many Bush administration officials does it take to change a lightbulb?

None. There's nothing wrong with that lightbulb. There is no need to change anything. We made the right decision and nothing has happened to change our minds. People who criticize this lightbulb now, just because it doesn't work anymore, supported us when we first screwed it in, and when these flip-floppers insist on saying that it is burned out, they are merely giving aid and encouragement to the Forces of Darkness.

**BUSHISM:**
"I hope you leave here and walk out and say, 'What did he say?'"

—Beaverton, Oregon, August 13, 2004

1. Lord, make this world to last as long as possible.

> —*Prayer of an eleven-year-old child,*
> *on hearing of Sino-Indian border fighting*

2. God, give us grace to accept with serenity the things that cannot be changed, courage to change the things that should be changed, and the wisdom to distinguish the one from the other.

> —*The Serenity Prayer Reinhold Niebuhr (1892–1971)*

3. Wherever I go, only Thou!
   Wherever I stand, only Thou!
   Just Thou, again Thou!
   Always Thou!
   Thou, Thou, Thou!
   When things are good, Thou!
   When things are bad, Thou!
   Thou, Thou, Thou!

> —*Early Hasidic song*

4. Lead me from death to life,
   from falsehood to truth.
   Lead me from despair to Hope,
   from fear to trust.
   Lead me from hate to love,
   from war to peace.
   Let Peace fill our hearts,
   our world, our universe.

> —*Satish Kumar, a member of the Jain community,*
> *as adapted by the Prayer for Peace movement, 1981*

5. In the time when God created all things, he created the sun.
   And the sun is born and dies and comes again.
   He created the moon,

And the moon is born and dies and comes again.
He created the stars,
And the stars are born and die and come again.
He created man.
And man is born and dies and comes not again.

*—Primal African prayer*
*Dinka, Sudan*

6. All that we ought to have thought and have not
    thought,
All that we ought to have said and have not said,
All that we ought to have done, and have not done;
All that we ought not to have thought, and yet have
    thought,
All that we ought not to have spoken, and yet have
    spoken,
All that we ought not to have done, and yet have
    done;
For thoughts, words and works, pray we, Oh God,
    for forgiveness.
And repent with penance.

*—Muslim, from an ancient Persian prayer*

7. Be present, O merciful God, and protect us through
    the silent hours of this night, so that we who are wea-
    ried by the changes and chances of this fleeting world
    may rest upon thy eternal changelessness; through
    Jesus Christ our Lord.

*—Ancient Collect at Compline, Book of Common Prayer*

8. When we live in Doubt,
        Grant us Faith.
    When we live in Despair,
        Grant us Hope.

> When we live in Death,
>     Grant us Love.
>
>                         —*Timothy Dobbins, 2004*

9. I will now develop the thought of loving-kindness towards the Three Noble Persons:

> An admired person: I extend loving-kindness towards him.
> A neutral person: I extend loving-kindness towards him.
> An enemy: I extend loving-kindness towards him.

When I have ended this meditation, should I still feel resentment against my enemy, then I will rebuke myself, saying: 'Fie upon you, ruthless one!
Has not the Blessed One said—' and I will repeat the parable of the saw.

Should I find that in spite of all my exertions I am not yet able to subdue my resentment, I will call to mind noble qualities in my enemy and reflect On them.

But should I still not be able to master my feeling, I will remember the Words of the Buddha, 'that this person too is the owner and heir of his deeds; that he is sprung from them, and that he will have his wholesome and unwholesome deeds as his inheritance.' In this way I will overcome hatred and feel compassion.

                     —*The Venerable Nyanatiloka, Buddhist monk,*
                                       *twentieth century*

# ACKNOWLEDGMENTS

This book could not have happened without the remarkable talents of the people at Random House. I don't actually know whom any of them voted for, but I like them regardless: my editor Jon Karp, my friend Don Weisberg, as well as Jillian Quint, Jonathan Jao, Elizabeth McGuire, Anthony Ziccardi, Thomas Perry, Barbara Fillon, Benjamin Dreyer, Lisa Feuer, and Gina Centrello.

I'd also like to thank all the contributors to this book who took time out of their hectic schedules to help: Anita Allen, Robert Anbian, Kurt Andersen, Gale Brewer, Tim Dobbins, Gail Evans, James Howe, Tracy Kidder, Mark Liponis, Jon Paul Newport, Judith Orloff, Russell Pearlman, Tim Sanders, Andrew Solomon, and Vicki Burns and everyone else at the Winnipeg Humane Society. Also, thanks go to James Stewart, Glenn Sinclair, Joel Kotkin, Alan Emtage, and Michael Rhodes, as well as the Bush Bible Squad: Carl Pritzkat, Tony Travostino, Christopher Barillas, Sarah Albert, and Miranda Spencer.

## ABOUT THE AUTHOR

GENE STONE, a former newspaper, magazine and book editor, has collaborated on more than twenty books and has written articles for *Esquire, GQ,* and *New York* magazine. A graduate of Stanford and Harvard universities, and a former Peace Corps volunteer, he lives in New York with his cat, a black-and-white Democrat named Gus.